INFORMATION COMPUTER COMMUNICATIONS POLICY

39

MOBILE CELLULAR COMMUNICATION

Pricing Strategies and Competition

ORGANISATION FOR ECONOMIC CO-OPERATION AND DEVELOPMENT

ORGANISATION FOR ECONOMIC CO-OPERATION AND DEVELOPMENT

Pursuant to Article 1 of the Convention signed in Paris on 14th December 1960, and which came into force on 30th September 1961, the Organisation for Economic Co-operation and Development (OECD) shall promote policies designed:

- to achieve the highest sustainable economic growth and employment and a rising standard of living in Member countries, while maintaining financial stability, and thus to contribute to the development of the world economy;
- to contribute to sound economic expansion in Member as well as non-member countries in the process of economic development; and
- to contribute to the expansion of world trade on a multilateral, non-discriminatory basis in accordance with international obligations.

The original Member countries of the OECD are Austria, Belgium, Canada, Denmark, France, Germany, Greece, Iceland, Ireland, Italy, Luxembourg, the Netherlands, Norway, Portugal, Spain, Sweden, Switzerland, Turkey, the United Kingdom and the United States. The following countries became Members subsequently through accession at the dates indicated hereafter: Japan (28th April 1964), Finland (28th January 1969), Australia (7th June 1971), New Zealand (29th May 1973), Mexico (18th May 1994) and the Czech Republic (21st December 1995). The Commission of the European Communities takes part in the work of the OECD (Article 13 of the OECD Convention).

Publié en français sous le titre :

LES COMMUNICATIONS CELLULAIRES MOBILES
Stratégies de tarification et concurrence

FOREWORD

This report was presented to the Telecommunications and Information Services Working Party (TISP) in June 1995 and was recommended to be made available to the public by the Information, Computer and Communications Policy (ICCP) Committee in October 1995.

At the same meeting, the ICCP agreed to the release of a statement entitled "OECD Reflections on the Benefits of Mobile Cellular Telecommunication Infrastructure Competition". This report formed the main background document for those reflections.

The report was prepared by Dr. Sam Paltridge of the OECD's Directorate for Science Technology and Industry. It is published on the responsibility of the Secretary-General of the OECD.

TABLE OF CONTENTS

LIST OF TABLES

LIST OF FIGURES

EXECUTIVE SUMMARY

There is a growing recognition in the OECD area of the importance of wireless communication for economic and social development. Mobile telecommunication is fast becoming an essential tool for business users seeking to boost efficiency in competitive markets and, increasingly, is being recognised as technology that can enable policy makers to reshape their vision of universal service. While much discussion of information infrastructure is devoted to the new services that can be delivered to business premises and homes, the value of mobile telecommunication largely rests on its ability to empower users outside these locations. Mobile telecommunication is not only proving its worth in an increasing range of business and public sector applications, but more recently for personal communication users in areas as diverse as convenience in social relations, personal security and public safety.

At the same time success in the development of services has not been uniform in the OECD area nor have the benefits been evenly distributed across different market structures. In fact the gap in performance between liberal and monopoly markets is growing, placing some countries at a critical disadvantage. For the first time a growing number of non-Member countries with competitive mobile telecommunication markets are outperforming many OECD countries with monopolies and duopolies. While some may believe that the necessary policy decisions have been taken by introducing a second operator, the relatively inefficient performance of countries with the longest experience with duopolies, and the benefits being achieved in more openly competitive markets, strongly suggest that momentum is building for a further wave of liberalisation.

The main message of this report is that competition is driving the growth of mobile telecommunication into new markets, particularly personal communication. The primary tool being used by operators in the first stage of openly competitive markets has been price differentiation. This has already had a dramatic impact on growth in the mobile subscriber base in competitive markets and increased the scope for new business and personal communication applications. If growth slows with current price settings, the new market structures being put into place in liberal countries will make them best placed to capture the next round of growth based on price competition. The primary findings of this report are:

- markets with infrastructure competition, and in particular where there is competition in both fixed and mobile networks, are delivering best practice performance in terms of market expansion;

- while there is evidence that monopoly markets are improved by the introduction of a second operator, developments in duopoly markets have been far from optimal, and substantial gains are being lost by delaying further liberalisation;

- it is in the interests of both incumbent operators, new market entrants, regulators and, most importantly, users, to have a clear separation between the operation of fixed and mobile network services;

- competitive mobile markets are delivering the most employment gains;

- universal service applications in mobile telecommunication are being enhanced by the use of competition;

- it would be highly desirable for regulators in the OECD area to develop a harmonised set of quality of service indicators for mobile communication, and for this information to be regularly reported.

INTRODUCING COMPETITION IN MOBILE MARKETS

Mobile communication is enjoying dynamic growth in the OECD area. In 1994 more than 1.2 million customers per month were added to mobile telecommunication networks (double the rate in 1992) and by year's end there were just over 44 million subscribers (Figure 1).[1] The recent surge in growth of mobile telecommunication, eclipsing what had previously been regarded as best practice, raises the question of why it has occurred and what lessons can be drawn from the experience of different Member countries. Success has not been uniform nor have the benefits been evenly distributed across different market structures. These issues are of pressing concern because policy makers are actively reviewing the structure of their mobile telecommunication markets. There is increasing recognition in a growing number of Member countries that far higher growth rates are possible if reforms to market structures, and in particular increased liberalisation, are implemented.[2]

For some it may seem the necessary decisions on market restructuring have already been taken, with most OECD countries having introduced, or being in the process of introducing, at least one additional mobile service provider.[3] By the beginning of 1995, a total of 16 countries had introduced a degree of competition in their mobile telecommunication market with most others set to follow shortly (Box 1). Between 1992 and 1994, 13 Member countries, including some that already had two mobile licensees, introduced additional operators. Those countries to introduce third and sometimes fourth operators include Australia, Canada, France, Germany, Japan, Sweden and the United Kingdom. In March 1995 the United States licensed up to six additional wireless operators in each market currently served by two mobile cellular providers. The actions of these countries, in going beyond duopolies, suggest a further wave of liberalisation is building momentum in the OECD area.

The main reason for the surge in the number of people using mobile telecommunication is the incentives competition has given to operators to expand the market. On the other hand, there is increasing evidence that monopolies, and to a slightly lessor extent duopolies, are not efficiently meeting demand for mobile telecommunication service or capturing the full benefits available. The available evidence is unambiguous in showing that competition is driving the growth of personal communication. Personal communication refers to the mass consumer market as distinct from business applications of mobile telecommunication. Where open competition has not been introduced it has proven to be the monopolists, and more recently the duopolists, that have been 'skimming the cream' from business users and ignoring the market for personal communication.

Figure 1. **Mobile telecommunication in the OECD**

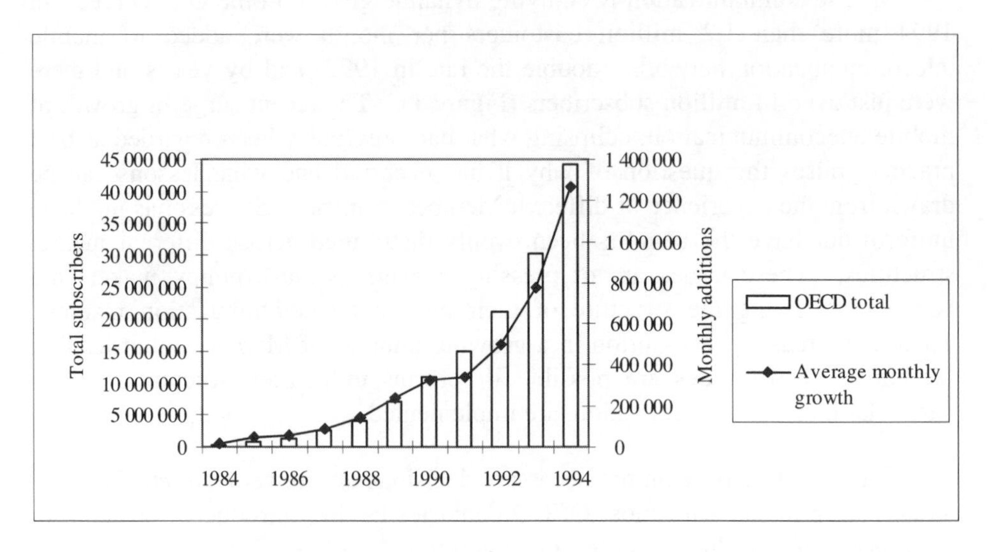

In those OECD countries without openly competitive markets it is demonstrable that the development of mobile communication is less than optimal. Substantial benefits are being lost not only by the contribution an efficient mobile telecommunication market can make for economic development, but in the social gains possible through the application of mobile telecommunication for universal service requirements, such as increasing the independence and security of the disabled or elderly. Indeed, in competitive markets operators are addressing precisely these types of users with 'low user schemes' priced in affordable ways. For a decade until 1992 this market had been ignored by monopoly and duopoly operators

For the achievement of the possible economic and social gains, experience has shown that liberalisation of the mobile telecommunication market is only a first step. A clear separation, either based on regulation or structural separation, of incumbent public switched telecommunication network (PSTN) operations and mobile operations has shown itself to be imperative. At the very least separation of accounts is a minimum requirement for a competitive market. This is not an onerous requirement. Operators should have this information as a matter of course to efficiently run their business, and a growing number of PTOs recognise structural separation (in the form of a spin-off company or independent subsidiary) best serves their interest in a competitive market. Moreover new mobile operators need efficient access to the PSTN, the right to invest in and construct their own infrastructure, and it is an increasingly recognised choice in the provider of fixed network infrastructure.

Box 1. Market Structure

The mobile telecommunication market in the OECD area can be broadly characterised into three groups. First is a group of nine Member countries that still have monopoly provision of mobile telecommunication services (Table 1). Some of these countries plan to introduce a competitor during 1995. Italy, the Netherlands and Spain have awarded second licences and service is expected toward the latter part of 1995. Second is a group of 11 countries that have a two operators in service. Most of these countries are relatively new to mobile telecommunication duopolies, with eight introducing a second operator since 1992. Two of these countries, France and New Zealand, have awarded the rights to operate a third mobile telecommunication service. Greece, the final country to introduce a mobile cellular service, opted to licence two new mobile operators (STET and Panafon) and has subsequently decided to allow OTE, the monopoly fixed link operator, to offer a third service if it wishes.[4] Canada and the United States, two countries with among the longest experience with mobile telecommunication duopolies, have licensed further operators. The first of Canada's new operators, Telezone, commenced service in early 1995 and MicroTel is initiating a PCS service trial.[5] In the United States AT&T, one of the many newly licensed PCS operators has announced it will commence service in the first half of 1997.[6] A third group of countries, Australia, Germany, Japan, Sweden and the United Kingdom had introduced three or more competitors by the end of 1994.

Table 1. **Mobile communication market structures in the OECD**

Market structure (1st Jan. 1995)	Country	Service commenced (Operators) 1st	2nd	3rd	4th	New entrants
Monopoly	Austria	1984				
	Iceland	1986				
	Luxembourg	1985				
	Switzerland	1987				
In transition	Belgium	1984				Licence to be awarded, 1995
	Netherlands	1989				1995
	Ireland	1985				Licence to be awarded, 1995
	Italy	1985				1995
	Spain	1982				1995
Duopoly	Denmark	1982	1992			
	Finland	1982	1992			
	Mexico	1989	1990			
	Norway	1981	1993			
	Portugal	1989	1992			
	Turkey	1986	1994			
In transition	France	1985	1992			3rd Operator - 1995
	Greece	1993	1993			Entry by OTE permitted
	New Zealand	1987	1993			3rd Operator Awarded
	United States	1984	1984			Multiple PCS licences
Open Market (3+)	Australia	1987	1992	1993		
	Canada	1985	1985	1995		4 entities licensed for CT2-Plus. PCS licences expected late 1995.
	Germany	1985	1992	1994		
	Japan	1979	1988	1994	1994	3 PCS licences for each of the 9 regions, 1995
	Sweden	1981	1981	1993		
	United Kingdom	1985	1985	1993	1994	

Source: OECD.

The fourth reason, and perhaps most crucial, is that competitive markets have proven best able to build significant growth beyond the business market. Competition is forcing operators to address new markets, and in doing so is driving the development of personal communication. This is why markets with open competition are generally not only growing much faster than monopoly and duopoly markets but changing the nature and characteristics of the subscriber base. The benefits of a competitive market have not only been proven in the field of service delivery but are increasingly seen as a vital link to the competitiveness of the manufacturing sector (Box 5).

Table 2. **Market structure and the growth of mobile telecommunication**

	Number of new mobile subscribers (monthly average)				
	1990	1991	1992	1993	1994
Australia	8 876	12 378	**20 750**	**40 500***	**87 000**
Austria	1 915	3 475	4 717	4 082*	4 768
Belgium	847	718	607	686	5 089*
Canada	**19 167**	**15 500**	**19 729**	**25 303**	**56 134**
Denmark	2 036	2 310	**2 543***	**12 739**	**12 590**
Finland	8 359	4 750	**3 730***	**10 784**	**13 531**
France	1 662	8 458	**4 542***	**7 919**	**28 493**
Germany	22 198	8 521	**37 479***	**65 498**	**55 168**
Greece	0	0	0	**1 417***	**11 083**
Iceland	197	219	251	126	382*
Ireland	702	800	783	742*	2 190
Italy	16 725	25 133	17 944*	35 239	86 065
Japan	**31 543**	**42 503**	**27 870**	**34 901**	**146 644**
Luxembourg	28	12	17	332*	598
Mexico	**5 467**	**8 708**	**11 783**	**6 150**	**15 017**
Netherlands	1 917	3 000	4 250	4 167	8 705*
New Zealand	2 675	942	1 725	**4 233***	**7 022**
Norway	2 431	2 575	5 432	**6 840***	**17 983**
Portugal	307	509	**2 058***	**5 331**	**6 023**
Spain	2 076	4 479	5 962	6 438	12 890
Sweden	**11 183**	**7 083**	**9 733***	**10 758**	**46 825**
Switzerland	4 359	4 121	3 375	3 558*	6 025
Turkey	1 350	1 335	1 131	1 900	**7 575***
United Kingdom	**15 833**	**7 917***	**20 583**	**63 250**	**130 222**
United States	**147 843**	**189 508**	**286 904**	**416 666**	**500 000**

1. Bold indicates the introduction of a second operator and shaded squares the introduction of a third or fourth operator. An asterisk indicates launch of digital service.

Source: OECD.

Box 2. Ranking comparative performance in mobile communication

Many reasons have been put forward to explain the relative position of Member countries in respect to mobile telecommunication penetration (refer section on comparative performance). Some, such as the date of service adoption, become less important as time passes, while others such as market structure become far more influential. Perhaps the most relevant comparison for countries is between early peers with similar economic, demographic and geographic characteristics. In other words if several countries were ranked at similar levels in 1987, it is pertinent to ask why this relationship had changed by 1994. The experience of the Nordic countries is a case in point. For example, was it the influence of competition from Sweden's duopoly which enabled it to surpass Norway's monopoly between 1988-89? Did the shift by Finland to a duopoly provide the stimulus to overtake Sweden in 1993 only to see the lead lost by the following year, after Sweden opted to introduce three competitors? Why has Iceland, with a monopoly, consistently lost ground to other Nordic countries and been overtaken by Australia and the United States? It is also notable that Denmark improved its position based on the stimulus of a second operator but has been overtaken by the outstanding performance of Australia with three operators.

Most countries with monopolies that have improved their performance, correlated with the introduction of digital service or in advance of competition, are generally still slipping relative to those with liberal markets. Switzerland is a prime example of a country which steadily improved its ranking until 1991, but has suffered a relative decline following the wave of liberalisation in other countries since 1992. Other monopolists to experience a decline in their ranking, despite recently improved performance, include Austria, Belgium, Ireland, the Netherlands and Spain. Luxembourg is an exception in that it has significantly improved its ranking. After faster growth in 1994, a year in advance of competition, Italy has shifted one position higher than 1990 by overtaking Austria.

Greece, after only three years of service with a competitive market, has a higher penetration rate than Belgium and Spain, after respectively eleven and twelve years of monopoly. Similarly Portugal has moved ahead of its early peers showing firm evidence for the benefits of competition. In 1992, a license to operate GSM technology was granted to a private operator -- Telecel. The other GSM licence was granted to the PTO already operating the analogue system. Portugal believes that, given its geography and demographics, the duopoly is performing at a high level but is leaving open the possibility of further market liberalisation. The only countries with competitive markets whose relative performance has been declining, France, Japan and Germany, have all taken action to further liberalise their markets. In the case of Japan and France this has already stabilised their ranking but, like the United Kingdom, they will be looking to this policy to increase performance after ending relatively unproductive duopolies. Similarly while the duopolies of Canada and the United States have been able to hold their positions roughly constant, fresh market openings should see their positions improve relative to other countries. In respect to Mexico, the early adoption of competition may be one factor in explaining why after five years of service, its penetration rate ranked ahead of ten other OECD countries at the same period. Similarly, the introduction of competition in Turkey has resulted in a large increase in monthly growth. Yet further gains, as evident in the experience of countries such as Malaysia and Thailand, are possible with increased liberalisation (Box 6).

Table 3. **Ranking mobile communication penetration in the OECD**

Rank	1987	1988	1989	1990	1991	1992	1993	1994
1	Norway	Norway	**Sweden**	**Sweden**	**Sweden**	**Sweden**	**Finland**	**Sweden**
2	**Sweden**	**Sweden**	Norway	Finland	Finland	**Finland**	**Sweden**	**Norway**
3	Iceland	Iceland	Finland	Norway	Norway	**Norway**	**Norway**	**Finland**
4	Denmark	Finland	Iceland	Iceland	Iceland	Iceland	**Denmark**	**Australia**
5	Finland	Denmark	Denmark	Denmark	Denmark	**US**	**Australia**	**Denmark**
6	**US**	**UK**	**UK**	**Canada**	**US**	**Denmark**	Iceland	**US**
7	**Canada**	**US**	**US**	**US**	**Canada**	**Australia**	**US**	Iceland
8	**UK**	**Canada**	**Canada**	**UK**	Switz.	**Canada**	**Canada**	**Canada**
9	Austria	Australia	Australia	Switz.	Australia	Switz.	**NZ**	**NZ**
10	Australia	Austria	Switz.	NZ	**UK**	NZ	**UK**	**UK**
11	Nether.	Switz.	NZ	Australia	NZ	**UK**	Switz.	Switz.
12	Japan	NZ	Austria	Austria	Austria	Austria	Austria	Italy
13	Ireland	Nether.	**Japan**	Italy	**Japan**	**Japan**	**Germany**	Austria
14	Switz.	Belgium	Ireland	**Japan**	Italy	Italy	Italy	Lux.
15	Germany	**Japan**	Nether.	Ireland	Ireland	**Germany**	**Japan**	**Germany**
16	Belgium	Ireland	Belgium	Germany	Nether.	Ireland	Nethe.	**Japan**
17	NZ	France	France	Nether.	Germany	Nether.	Ireland	Ireland
18	France	Germany	Germany	Belgium	Belgium	**France**	Lux.	Nether.
19	Lux.	Lux.	Italy	France	France	Belgium	**Portugal**	**Portugal**
20	Italy	Italy	Lux.	Lux.	Spain	Spain	**France**	**France**
21	Spain	Spain	Spain	Spain	Lux.	**Portugal**	Belgium	**Greece**
22	Turkey	Turkey	Turkey	**Mexico**	**Mexico**	**Mexico**	Spain	Belgium
23			Portugal	Portugal	Portugal	Lux.	**Mexico**	Spain
24				Turkey	Turkey	Turkey	**Greece**	**Mexico**
25						**Greece**	Turkey	**Turkey**

1. Bold indicates the introduction of a second operator and shaded squares the introduction of a third or fourth operator.

Source: OECD

Competition and personal communication

Recently mobile telecommunication has reached a major turning point by breaking out of the business market into the realm of personal communication. In the first decade of its development, 1982-92, mobile telecommunication was overwhelmingly led by business demand. Many businesses were prepared to pay high prices for service, relative to the fixed network, because they recognised the importance mobile telecommunication could have for improving efficiency. By the same token the advantages of mobile telecommunication were clearly not important to all firms, or to the tasks of all employees, and certainly not at premium prices.[11]

The initial demand for mobile telecommunication came from people whose job required mobility (*e.g.* travelling sales, transport, trades people) but had to be in permanent contact with others (*e.g.* office, suppliers, customers). As most mobile users already had a fixed telephone line, initial demand came from the development of a new market. Nevertheless this market was still only a relatively small part of the overall market for business communication. One indication of business demand for fixed telecommunication service is the number of mainlines connected to business premises. This measure is less reliable than it once was because of the use of private branch exchanges in business premises and the increasing number of home workers. Nevertheless it is one benchmark against which to place into perspective business demand for mobile telecommunication. For example in the United Kingdom, there was 10.8 mobile subscribers per 100 business mainlines in March 1989. Over the following two years this ratio doubled to be 20.1 mobile subscribers per 100 business mainlines by March 1991. However in the next two years the ratio only increased to be 22.2 business mobile subscribers per 100 business mainlines by March 1993. In large part this is due to a general slow-down of economic activity during this period but it was also clear that in an increasingly competitive environment operators had to address new markets.

Charging relatively high prices to business users resulted in spectacular profit margins for many public telecommunication operators (PTOs), sometimes more than 40 per cent of mobile turnover, but this was an impediment to the expansion of service beyond a limited range of applications within the business market. In other words, PTOs that charged high prices from the vantage of monopoly, and sometimes duopoly, markets were skimming the cream! The profitability of mobile telecommunication was generally not transparent because the accounts of most PTOs had no separate line for mobile telecommunication.

Of course the high price of handsets also deterred personal communication users, who could not claim the cost as a tax deduction for business purposes. Yet the high cost was directly related, by today's standards, to the relatively low volume of handsets purchased from manufacturers. In 1994 sales of mobile handsets in the OECD were nearly four times greater than 1991.

Even though the expansion of mobile telecommunication was relatively slow in the decade before 1992, compared to post 1992, its pace was still far ahead of most expectations. During the 1980s, most PTOs seriously underestimated the strength of demand for mobile telecommunication and as a result their business plans were askew. The main reason for this was a business culture that derived from an era when telecommunication was not a demand-led industry. Instead of prioritising resources for the mobile communication services business customers wanted, PTOs sometimes invested in other business services ahead of demand (*e.g.* ISDN). This trend sometimes reflected differences within PTOs about the future direction of telecommunication with some fixed link divisions fearful about how the new service would impact on them. This may be one reason the pricing of mobile telecommunication in many countries appeared to be much higher than justified by cost. On the other hand this may have reflected the judgement of PTOs, based on a low projected growth rates, that mobile telecommunication was a low-volume high-profit market.

The fact that demand outstripped expectations meant that there was little incentive to market services in an efficient way. PTOs seemed content with the demand they had not envisaged rather than seeking a vision of new demand. For example, the pricing of mobile telecommunication was undertaken on a uniform basis and little differentiation was made for potential users with contrasting usage patterns (*e.g.* corporations, small business users, personal communication users). As a result many of the personal communication applications increasingly evident in a social context (*e.g.* security, safety, convenience) did not develop. However the wave of liberalisation between 1992 and 1994 has radically impacted on this situation.

Incumbent operators have torn up pre-existing business and investment plans. In the same way that the advent of companies such as MCI and Sprint forced AT&T to bring forward digitalisation of its network, competition is now driving mobile operators to expand capacity and upgrade their networks at a faster pace than originally planned. For example Cellnet "...will be spending about a million pounds a day upgrading its GSM network in the United Kingdom. This is not geographical coverage -- Cellnet already claims to have 98 per cent population coverage -- but capacity spend. The network will be optimised for hand-portables and deep in-building coverage, it will incorporate minicells and use new base station and antenna designs to minimise environmental impact, it will add another 1 400 base stations to the 1 050 already in place ... By the end of 1996, Cellnet will be delivering the capacity they had previously planned to reach by 2002. The strategy clearly seems to be targeting the mass consumer market."[12]

The stimulus provided by new operators is forcing incumbents to be more responsive to the needs of existing customers and address new markets. Arguably, the greatest benefit from the introduction of competition in mobile telecommunication to date has not been price reductions, although it has certainly brought price discipline to many markets, but in forcing operators to diversify their tariffs in search of new markets. Demand for the range of new tariffs has been little short of phenomenal. For example, in 1993 when Cellnet introduced its "Lifetime" package in the United Kingdom, 107 000 customers took advantage of the offer compared to an increase of only 4 000 new customers for existing tariff options aimed at business users. In addition some existing customers were able to migrate to different tariff packages that better suited their needs.

These developments are already changing the character of the mobile telecommunication market and enhancing social development. For example in Canada the number of women with mobile telephones is growing much more rapidly that the overall market. In 1991 women comprised 17 per cent of Bell Mobility Cellular's customers, increasing to 19 per cent by 1992.[13] However by mid-1994 women comprised nearly 28 per cent of Bell Mobility Cellular's customers. Moreover additions to the network are taking on seasonal characteristics of commodity products with the pre-Christmas periods of 1993 and 1994 setting new records in several OECD countries. In Australia, with three mobile operators, well over 100 000 mobile customers were added to analogue and digital networks in December 1994. This was nearly as many customers as were added over the whole of the last full financial year of monopoly provision in 1990/91.

Marketing in a competitive telecommunication environment has a vastly different character from the traditional monopoly approach of PTOs. Mobile communication operators sell a range of value added services designed to make the service a more efficient tool for users. Examples of supplementary services also found on the PSTN include call barring, call forwarding, call hold, call waiting, and voice mail. However in competitive markets operators are providing innovative service not generally available over fixed networks. In the United Kingdom, a consumer buying a mobile service from Orange Personal

Communications could for the payment of a £75 fee select their date of birth as their personal telephone number. While this may seem frivolous to some, memorable telephone numbers are a high priority for certain personal communication users and many business users. Indeed, Orange has one option aimed at business to enable users to choose highly memorable numbers for their own customers (*e.g.* 0973 222 222).[14]

Where competition has not been introduced, or where operators have been sheltered by a duopoly, pricing and service innovation has been much slower to emerge. In many monopoly markets there is still one uniform tariff for all customers. By way of contrast the introduction of new competitors quickly focuses existing operators' attention on improving and expanding service. In the United Kingdom, after eight years of operation in a duopoly, Vodafone and Cellnet introduced flexible tariff options just prior to the launch of One-2-One and Orange. In the United States, AirTouch, a leading provider of cellular services began targeting the consumer market with special promotions and pricing plans in the second half of 1994.[15] AirTouch also expanded marketing into consumer electronics stores and other mass market distribution channels. This new strategy emerged after ten years of duopoly service, just prior to the issuing of licences for new PCS competitors. In all these cases leading cellular firms operating in duopolies did not create new strategies for the expansion of personal communication until they faced an increasingly competitive market.

Operators in competitive markets have also addressed the cost of handsets as an impediment to non-business users joining mobile networks. In the United Kingdom during March 1995, it was possible to buy a mobile telephone for US$15 including sales tax and join a network with the connection charge waived. The recommended retail price for this handset was US$124 and the saving on a normal connection fee was up to US$109. Service providers were able to provide these prices because network operators paid bonuses for every new customer. They, in turn, recouped the bonus from higher rental and usage charges. Similarly in the United States, where accounts of mobile companies have separate lines for equipment sales, it can be observed that operators lose money on the sale of equipment because they sell it at or below cost. For AirTouch the cost of equipment sales (revenues from sales of cellular telephones) was greater than revenue from equipment sales in 1993 and 1994 (Table 4). Moreover AirTouch expects that the contribution margins of retail equipment sales will remain negative as it responds to competitive market pressure.[16] Nevertheless the company was able to increase the profitability of its United States operations, despite falling revenue per subscriber. One factor contributing to this trend is that the cost of revenues declined as a percentage of net operating revenues, reflecting economies of scale as network costs are spread over a larger subscriber base, and other efficiency gains.

The new tariff options and marketing strategies, innovations brought about by competition, are driving growth in the personal communication market where users have a range of needs apart from business applications. Since targeting the personal communication market in 1994, AirTouch reports that this segment is now generating most of its subscriber growth. One indicator of this trend is the declining revenue per subscriber which the company attributes to the tendency for personal communication users (particularly those on low-use tariff options) to make less calls than business users (Table 4).

Table 4. **AirTouch domestic (United States) proportionate cellular operating results**

US$ million

	1992	1993	1994
Service & other revenues	699.4	892.0	1 149.6
Equipment sales	24.8	40.2	74.6
Cost of equipment sales	(23.9)	(42.2)	(82.0)
Net operating revenues	700.3	890.0	1 142.2
Cost of revenues	98.7	116.3	126.0
Selling, general & administrative expenses	322.5	394.1	537.2
Depreciation and amortisation	124.1	164.7	185.7
Total operating expenses	545.3	675.1	848.9
Operating income	155.0	214.9	293.3
Other indicators & financial data			
Operating cash flow(1)	279.1	379.6	479.0
Capital expenditures, excluding acquisitions	199.8	198.4	296.7
Operating income as per cent of service & other revenue	22.2	24.1	25.5
Proportionate cellular subscribers (number) (2)	744 000	1 046 000	1 560 000
Revenue per subscriber (US$)	940.0	852.7	736.9

1. Operating cash flow is defined as operating income plus depreciation and amortisation.
2. Proportionate subscriber data is obtained from each system over which the company has or shares operational control, by multiplying *(i)* the aggregate number of subscribers to such system; and *(ii)* the Company's ownership interest in each system. Proportionate subscriber data does not include subscribers to systems over which the Company does not have or share operational control.

Source: AirTouch.

In Italy a tariff option for personal communication introduced by Telecom Italia, after a government decision to issue a second licence, has had a major impact on the growth of mobile subscribers. In less than two years the new tariff option attracted more customers than ten years of tariffs aimed at business users (Table 5). In 1994 subscriber growth per capita was four times what it had been in 1992. While the improved performance by Telecom Italia has been impressive, assisted by the pending entry of a second operator, further benefits can be achieved. Italy's subscriber growth still lags behind most competitive markets and can be expected to be boosted by the launch of a second operator in 1995.

In 1994 Cellnet was signing up four customers on personal tariffs to every one customer on business tariffs (Table 6). For Vodafone the ratio was six to one, albeit the digital service launched in December 1991 was beginning to attract significant numbers of business users for the first time. Flemmings Research projects that the mobile subscriber base in the United Kingdom will grow from 3.5 million at the end of 1994 to 10 to 15 million by the year 2000.[17] They expect 75 per cent of growth will be generated by the personal communication sector (Figure 2).

Table 5. **New tariff options and mobile subscriber growth in Italy**

	1993				1994			
	1st Q	2nd Q	3rd Q	4th Q	1st Q	2nd Q	3rd Q	4th Q
Business subscribers	829 452	876 410	892 819	904 321	923 690	967 227	1 009 260	1 055 178
Personal subscribers	0	32 128	150 883	302 630	457 117	697 160	929 216	1 184 560
Business (per cent)	100	96.5	85.5	74.9	66.9	58.1	52.1	47.1
Personal (per cent)	0	3.5	14.5	25.1	33.1	41.9	47.9	52.9

Source: OECD.

Table 6. **Mobile telecommunication subscriber growth and flexible tariff options in the United Kingdom**

Operator	Tariff option	Mar.1991	Mar.1992	Mar.1993	Mar.1994	Dec. 1994
Cellnet	Business anal.	509 000	547 000	551 000	688 000	792 000
	Personal	0	0	107 000	331 000	756 000
	Digital	0	0	0	0	15 000
Vodafone	Business anal.	656 000	713 000	753 000	917 000	977 000
	Personal	0	0	85 000	235 000	543 000
	Digital	0	n.a.	n.a.	22 000	118 000
One-2-One	PCS	0	0	0	73 000	205 000
Orange	PCS	0	0	0	0	100 000
Total Subscribers	All tariffs	1 165 000	1 260 000	1507000	2 266 000	3 506 000
Monthly Average	All tariffs	16 000	8 000	21 000	63 000	130 000

Source: BT, Vodafone, Robert Flemming, Oftel, OECD.

Figure 2. **Actual and Projected Mobile Subscribers in the UK**

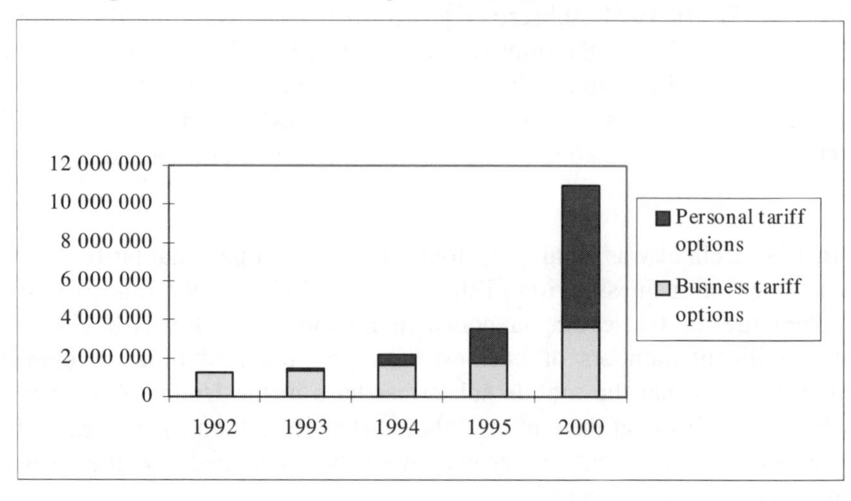

The growth in the market for personal communication has also been a welcome development for business users. Indeed, some personal communication tariff options are attractive to certain types of business users. Nevertheless the main gains from an increasingly competitive market are that operators are having to address new business markets. An example is a tariff option that allows a user to be charged at rates comparable to, or less than, the fixed network in a certain place of their choice (*e.g.* office, home) but at the usual mobile rates outside that location. Accordingly, to continue with the example of the United Kingdom, the growth of business mobile subscribers per cent business mainlines has returned to pre-recession rates. By March 1994 there was nearly 37 mobile subscribers per 100 business mainlines, of which 26 per cent were subscribing to tariff options aimed at business.

As recognition increases that efficient telecommunication is a key to economic and social development, the governments of OECD countries with monopolies, or inefficient duopolies, will face a stark choice. Either they introduce more open markets or face slipping further behind the pace setters. It should not be overlooked, based on improved achievements due to other factors, that competition is widening the performance gap between OECD countries. Some countries are harnessing competitive forces to take full advantage of the capability of mobile communication to enhance economic and social development. Other countries that have been slower to come to terms with the dynamics of this market are missing substantial gains. Moreover in an increasingly competitive global market it is notable that a number of non-Member countries, as diverse as Hong Kong, Malaysia and Thailand, are outperforming many OECD countries with monopolies (Box 6).

Box 3. PCS auctions in the United States

In issuing additional licences to provide mobile telecommunication services, governments in the OECD have adopted a number of different selection procedures. In respect to the management of the radio spectrum and licensing the issues raised were discussed by the Information, Computer and Communications Policy Committee (ICCP) in 1992. Subsequently a report was published on *The Economics of Radio Frequency Allocation* which had as one of its major conclusions that spectrum should be allocated by competitive bidding backed up by regulatory safeguards and licensing obligations.[18] The United States has been one Member country to adopt this approach in 1993, when the United States Congress authorised the Federal Communications Commission (FCC) to conduct spectrum auctions. Since that time four auctions have been held which have raised a total of US$8.9 billion for the US Treasury or about US$98 per United States' household.

In March 1995 the largest of these auctions, and in fact the largest auction of United States government assets in history, was completed by the FCC. The auction raised US$7.7 billion for the US Treasury. On offer were 99 licences to provide PCS across the United States and its territories.[19] Prior to the auction there were two providers of mobile cellular telecommunication in each region of the United States. After the series of auctions there could be as many as eight wireless providers in each market, made up of the two existing operators and six new PCS operators. The auction process was completed in record time. Under a previous system using lottery it took more than a year from the initial application to licence grant.[20] When licences were granted by comparative hearings, the process often took several years.

Table 7. **Largest United States PCS licence winners**

Company	Partners	Population covered (millions)	Amount paid (US$m)	Price per potential subscriber (US$)
WirelessCo	Comcast, Cox Cable, Sprint, TCI	145	2 110	14.56
AT&T	AT&T	107	1 684	15.73
PCS Primeco	AirTouch/US West Bell Atlantic/Nynex	57	1 107	19.36
PacTel	PacTel	31	696	22.41
TDS	TDS	26	288	11.10
GTE Macro	GTE	19	398	20.56
Western PCS	Western Wireless, John Stanton	14	144	10.49
Bell South	Bell South	11	82	7.15
Powertel PCS	Rural Telco	9	124	13.85
PhillieCo	Cox, Sprint, TCI	9	85	9.52

Source: Merrill Lynch, *Communicationsweek International.*

Box 4. Employment in mobile communication

Mobile telecommunication is one of the fastest growing areas of telecommunication employment. At a time when most PTOs in the OECD area are reducing the size of their workforce, mobile telecommunication had generated more than 90 000 jobs in network operators by 1992.[21] In April 1994, the OECD made available to the public a report entitled *Employment Restructuring in Public Telecommunication Operators* [OCDE/GD(95)99] which updated the information available on mobile telecommunication and employment. That report showed a positive link between market liberalisation in mobile telecommunication and the growth in employees, and took as examples the experience in Australia, Japan and the United Kingdom after the shift beyond duopoly markets (Figures 3, 4 and 5).

Figure 3. **Mobile subscriber growth and employment trends in Australia**

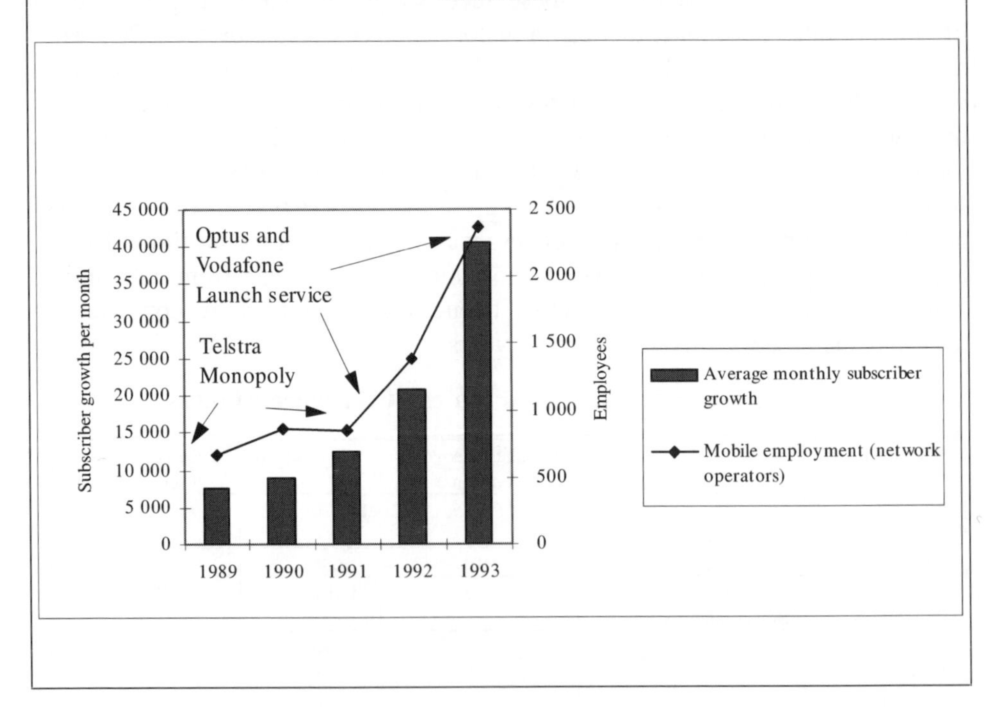

Figure 4. **Mobile subscriber growth in Japan and NTT mobile employment**

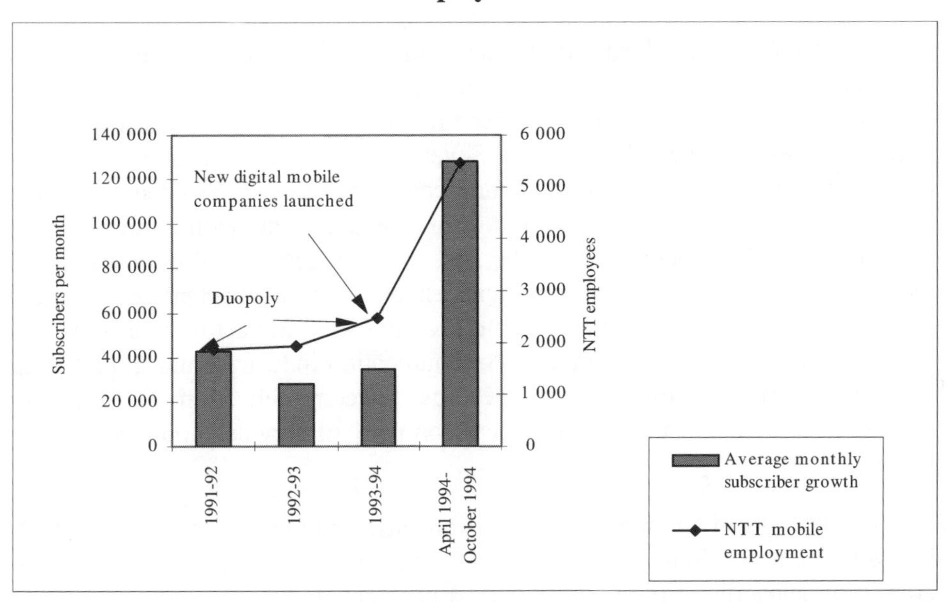

Figure 5. **UK mobile subscriber and employment trends after the duopoly**

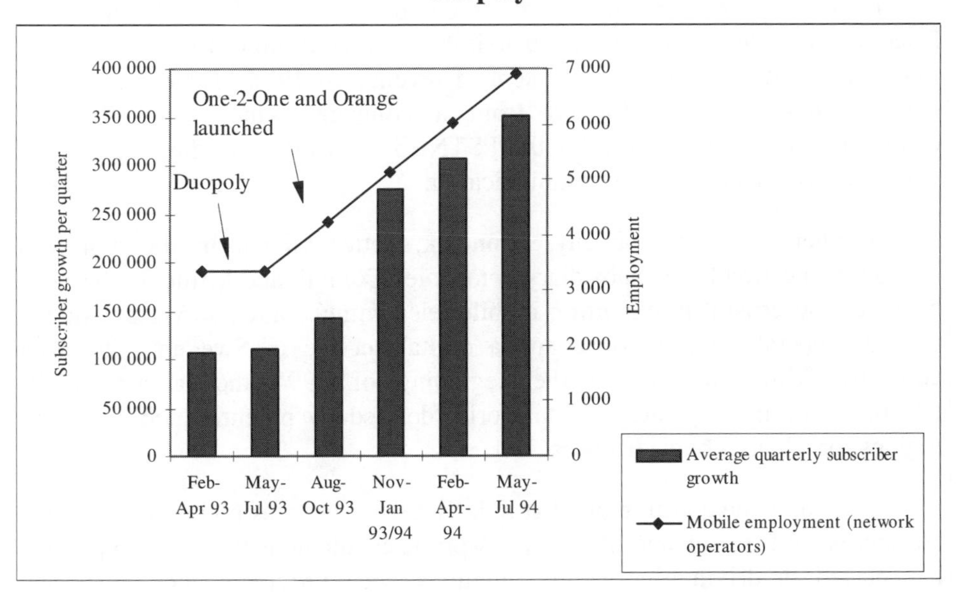

Box 5. Services policy, manufacturing and export growth in Sweden: LM Ericsson and Kinnevik

Sweden has been a leader in the development of mobile telecommunication with the first service introduced by Telia in 1981. By 1994 Sweden had the highest mobile telecommunication penetration rate, and the fastest growing subscriber base, in the OECD area. Several reasons have been forwarded to explain the rapid development of mobile communication in Sweden including, in respect to communication policy, the first 'experiment' with competition in the early 1980s and being among the first to introduce a third operator in the 1990s.[22] To the extent that these policies encouraged the efficient development of the services market it is interesting to examine what impact they have had on directly related sectors of the mobile communication industry: and in particular on the performance of Sweden's leading telecommunication manufacturer L.M. Ericsson, and Kinnevik, the parent company of service suppliers Comvik and Millicom.

In the field of mobile communication infrastructure by the end of 1994, Ericsson systems were installed in 74 countries and used by more than 20 million subscribers (slightly above 40 per cent of the world market).[23] In 1994 sales of mobile telecommunication systems and terminals rose 73 per cent and profits in Ericsson's mobile operations were reported to be 'very strong' contributing to an 80 per cent increase in company wide profits. The growth of Ericsson's mobile operations has made it the main contributor to the company's sales after providing only 15 per cent of revenue in 1988 (Table 8). In fact Ericsson has been transformed from a company which primarily sold communication infrastructure for the PSTN to the world's leading supplier of wireless networks for mobile communication.

Another Swedish company, Kinnevik, better known in the world of telecommunication by its subsidiary companies Comvik and Millicom, has also been very successful in exporting mobile telecommunication services. Comvik currently operates an analogue and a digital service in Sweden. Its sister company, Millicom was by the beginning of 1994 the largest mobile telecommunication operator in the world, defined by potential subscribers in regions for which it holds licences.[24]

This raises the question of what link Sweden's services policy has had with the success of Ericsson and Millicom. A prime candidate is the role competition has played in driving innovation among service providers and consequent demands for innovation among manufacturers. This is highlighted by the fact that 60 per cent of Ericsson's net sales in 1994 were attributable to products which did not exist in 1991. In Sweden much of the drive comes from the need for service suppliers to innovate in a competitive market. A case in point is Telia's order to Ericsson for the world's first dual mode GSM/DECT telephones with delivery scheduled for the beginning of 1996. The dual mode terminals can be used on any GSM (Global System for Mobile Communications) network in the world as well as DECT (Digital European Cordless Telecommunications) networks installed on business premises. When used by customers the handsets automatically choose the DECT network if coverage is available or the GSM network if DECT it is not available. It could be pointed out that sales in Sweden made up less than 10 per cent of Ericsson's total world sales such that domestic policy was only a relatively small influence. However the company is receiving similar demand in other liberal markets. A similar dual mode GSM/DECT service trial is being initiated with Detemobil in Germany, while the main boost to sales in OECD countries in 1994 came from the most liberal countries -- Australia, Japan, the United Kingdom and United States.

Millicom's success in winning 19 licences outside of Sweden by 1994 (the next largest was Bell South with 12 international licences) has been based on Kinnevik's 14 years of experience in the Swedish market. Comvik, which entered the Swedish mobile telecommunication market in 1981, was the first competitor to Telia. When a digital licence was offered in 1989 Comvik's long involvement yielded a GSM licence. Millicom's business strategy on the other hand involves applying for licences and then constructing and managing networks outside the Nordic region, the United Kingdom and United States. Millicom reports its various licences generally show a profit after 24 months compared to four years for western countries.[25] In the case of both Ericsson and Kinnevik, Sweden's policy of domestic liberalisation in services has helped foster export-oriented companies that are leaders in related mobile communication sectors.

Table 8. **Contribution of radio communications to LM Ericsson sales**

	1988	1989	1990	1991	1992	1993	1994
Radio communications (SEKm)	4 745	8 062	11 693	12 420	15 040	25 956	40 940
Total sales (SEKm)	31 297	38 549	45 702	46 000	47 000	62 954	82 554
Radio communications as per cent of total	15	21	26	27	32	41	50

Source: LM Ericsson, Datapro.

Comparative performance

Given that the OECD area has a decade of experience with mobile telecommunication (average date of launch - 1985), it would seem timely to compare the relative performance of different market structures. Several criteria could be used for such comparisons such as price, innovation and quality of service. Price, and innovation in pricing, is considered in the section on tariffs. While an assessment of quality of service would be useful, little data is available of a comparative nature. Few countries report quality of service data for mobile communication although operators have, or should have, this data readily available for their own network and business management purposes. It would be highly desirable for regulators in the OECD area to define a number of key indicators for quality of service in mobile telecommunication and for this information to be published on a regular basis. For example, in Australia data is available on the mobile call drop out rate at national level and this is reported on a six-monthly basis.[26] Austel, the Australian regulatory authority, also examines data for particular problem areas (*e.g.* the central business district of major cities) and requires explanations from operators if performance slips below accepted standards. Oftel, the United Kingdom regulatory authority, is one of the few authorities to have carried out an independent survey of quality of service.

In the absence of other data, most analysis of mobile telecommunication in different countries contains a comparison of the mobile subscriber penetration rate (Table 9). Countries with a high mobile penetration rate are generally viewed as having performed better than those with low equivalents. Accordingly, countries such as Sweden, Norway and Finland are viewed as leaders in the development of mobile services. It is also true that these countries were among the first to offer service, meaning they have had a longer time to develop networks and build the number of subscribers. Yet, while the date of service launch may be a significant factor in understanding the penetration of mobile subscribers in some countries, it is not a complete guide to performance. Why by 1995, for example, did Greece, after only two years of service, have a higher mobile telephone penetration rate that Austria and Spain after more than ten years of service? The success of some countries derives directly from the quality of performance rather than the length of service.

Table 9 contains a comparison of monthly subscriber growth weighted by population. Growth was calculated on a monthly basis so that it allowed comparisons between countries with different reporting dates. The 1994 monthly growth rates are illustrated in Figure 6. Here it can be observed that the development gap between some OECD countries is growing. For example,

Sweden and Australia with competitive mobile markets and PSTN infrastructure competition have a rate of growth that is more than ten times that of some other Member countries. Yet, as the experience of several countries shows, this does not have to be the case. For example, even though Japan has a lower penetration rate than Austria, its subscriber base is growing three times as fast. Similarly Greece with a quarter of Switzerland's penetration rate was able to generate much faster growth in 1994. Clearly Member countries can change their performance levels if they reform policy settings.

While a range of factors were influential in the initial take up of services, with early success being enjoyed in a mixture of market structures, they are no longer crucial in explaining why some countries are performing relatively better than others. Nevertheless it is useful to consider the major factors which have been forwarded to explain the initial growth rates in different market structures, because the primary thesis of this report is that competition is now the key factor driving market development. Many explanations, apart from the liberalisation of mobile telecommunication, have been offered for the different rates of development in Member countries, including the existing efficiency of the operators of fixed networks upon which mobile communication is dependent; the regulatory environment pertaining to the fixed network; the relative wealth of the population and their acceptance of new technology; the cost and pricing of service; and the date of adoption (*i.e.* length of service); the influence government regulation may have had on the geographical coverage achieved; the demographic features of a country, including whether a high proportion of leisure time is spent outside cities, including in small boats and cabins; and, in the case of Scandinavia, the roaming capability enabled by the adoption of the NMT system. The aim of this analysis is to show that while these factors may have been influential in the past, they need not be constraints for the future.

Figure 6. **Mobile penetration and growth**

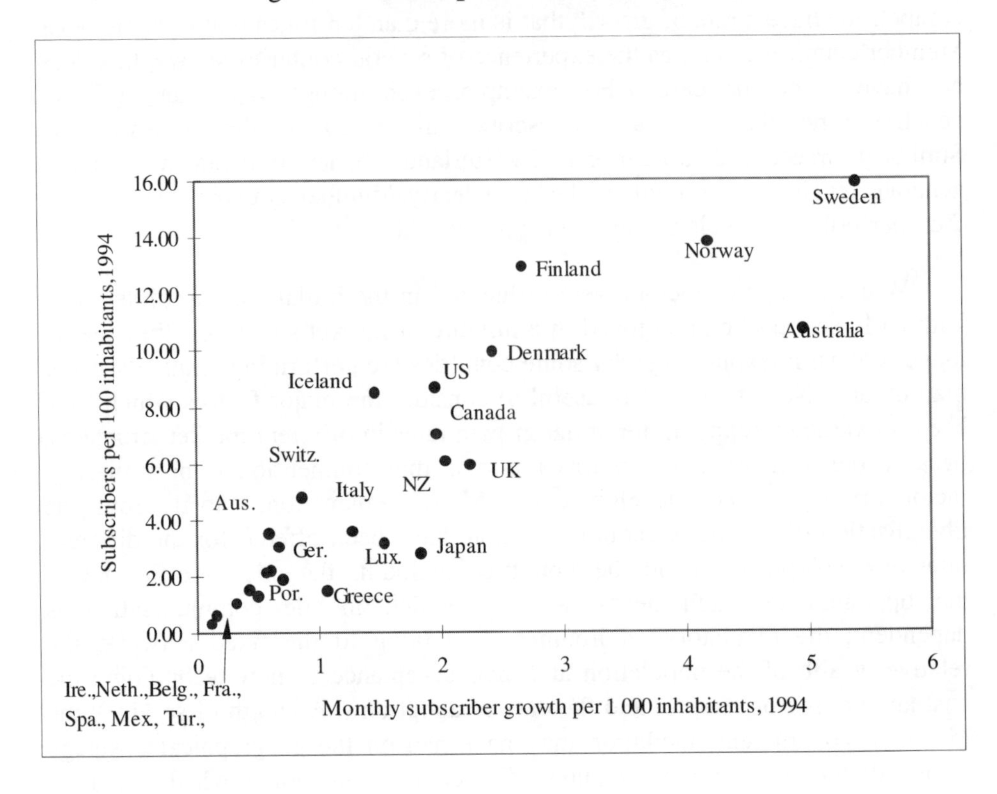

Table 9. **Mobile telecommunication penetration and growth in the OECD area**

Country	Mobile subscribers (1 January 1995)	Subscribers per 1 000 inhabitants	Average monthly subscriber additions per 1 000 inhabitants				
			1990	1991	1992	1993	1994
Australia(1)	1 871 000	106.70	0.51	0.71	1.18	2.31	4.96
Austria	278 200	35.29	0.24	0.44	0.60	0.52	0.60
Belgium	128 000	12.74	0.08	0.07	0.06	0.07	0.51
Canada	2 000 000	70.30	0.67	0.55	0.69	0.89	1.97
Denmark	510 396	98.72	0.39	0.45	0.49	2.46	2.44
Finland	651 551	129.22	1.66	0.94	0.74	2.14	3.58
France	803 935	14.01	0.03	0.15	0.21	0.22	0.43
Germany	2 430 000	30.16	0.28	0.11	0.47	0.81	0.68
Greece	150 000	14.56	0.00	0.00	0.00	0.14	1.08
Iceland	22 000	84.62	0.76	0.84	0.96	0.49	1.96
Ireland	76 185	21.48	0.20	0.23	0.22	0.21	0.62
Italy	2 240 000	39.40	0.29	0.44	0.31	0.62	1.5
Japan	3 450 800	27.80	0.25	0.34	0.22	0.28	1.83
Luxembourg	12 253	31.42	0.07	0.03	0.04	0.85	1.53
Mexico	565 500	6.65	0.06	0.10	0.14	0.07	0.18
Netherlands	320 458	22.39	0.13	0.20	0.28	0.27	0.57
New Zealand	207 000	60.12	0.78	0.27	0.50	1.23	2.04
Norway	590 799	137.81	0.57	0.60	1.27	1.60	4.19
Portugal	173 508	17.60	0.03	0.05	0.21	0.54	0.61
Spain	411 930	10.54	0.05	0.11	0.15	0.16	0.33
Sweden	1 376 000	158.64	1.29	0.82	1.12	1.24	5.40
Switzerland	330 000	48.00	0.63	0.60	0.49	0.52	0.88
Turkey	175 089	2.96	0.02	0.02	0.02	0.03	0.17
United Kingdom	3 438 000	59.43	0.24	0.17	0.36	1.09	2.25
United States	22 000 000	86.00	0.58	0.74	1.13	1.62	1.96

1. Data for Australia for 1994 is February 1995. At the end of 1994 there were 1 567 725 analogue subscribers and approximately 130 000 digital subscribers for Telstra, Optus and Vodafone. End of February data, which was the latest available at the time of writing, is used to smooth seasonal variations. Population data is used for the purpose of weighting is 1992.

Source: OECD, CTIA, Public Networks Europe.

Efficiency of fixed network operators

The initial operators of mobile telecommunication were overwhelmingly the PTOs responsible for the PSTN, so their relative efficiency is a natural starting point for analysis of performance. While there can be many different approaches to gauging relative efficiency, the tele-density of a country is a reasonable benchmark to use when considering the roll out of mobile services. In other words if a country has achieved a good record in provision of the fixed network it might be expected that they would have repeated this performance in mobile communication.

For the development of a new service, the PTO can be assumed to have many of the same national challenges or comparative advantages faced in past development. Many caveats could be raised in relation to this proposition. For example policy reform over the past several years, such as separation of regulation from operation and the new managerial independence this entails for operators, means that many PTOs should have been starting without certain disadvantages confronted in the past. Moreover access to capital, sometimes a problem for state-owned PTOs facing heavy demands from the fixed network, should not have been an obstacle for the development of mobile services given the very high returns on offer. If lack of capital has been a barrier to mobile development in any OECD country that problem and the solution is patently in the domain of policy makers.

Second, the efficiency of the fixed network on which mobile telecommunication is still dependent for most transmission, call completion and call origination is a crucial input for the subsidiaries of PTOs or other mobile operators. It could also be suggested that an inefficient operator, with a low quality of service and long waiting list, may prompt faster growth in mobile telecommunication. This is less likely to apply to OECD countries because of their relatively modern networks, in terms of the deployment of new technologies, and low waiting lists. Moreover the relatively high price of mobile service compared to the fixed network is likely to minimise this trend particularly in countries with low per capita incomes. Therefore it is a reasonable assumption that those PTOs with an efficient PSTN service should have been expected to have repeated this with mobile telecommunication.

In practice, while some relatively efficient incumbent PTOs have been able to build on their past PSTN performance (represented here in proxy to be higher tele-density), others have not been able to accomplish this feat (Figure 7). The extreme range in performance for countries with more than 40 mainlines per 100 people is remarkable particularly for those with roughly the same fixed network penetration. For example for those countries above 60 mainlines per 100 people, the difference between Sweden and Switzerland or Luxembourg is very large. For those countries between 50 and 60 mainlines per 100 people, there are also very great differences between countries such as Norway and France. Similarly between 40 and 50 mainlines per 100 people there are vast differences between Australia and the Netherlands, or New Zealand and Belgium.

At the same time some countries with low tele-densities have been able to perform better than would have been expected based on a consideration of this measure alone. This raises the question of why, for example, Portugal has outperformed Belgium, France and Spain even though it has a lower tele-density. Similarly why has Mexico been able to develop service faster than Turkey? Obviously this is presenting a static comparison of performance and the date of service introduction needs to be taken into account. Nevertheless, without pre-empting later discussion, it is pertinent to note that Portugal commenced service five years, and Greece eight years, after Belgium.

Given the range of performance a number of conclusions can be drawn. Most obvious is that there are other factors at work in the initial performance of operators. While it could be surmised that tele-density does not correlate with efficiency in a way that impacts on mobile development, there is a more likely explanation. In those countries with a performance lower than expectations, but more than one operator, it is rather the case that competitors did not have efficient access to the existing networks. For those countries with a monopoly, or without competition until recently, the correlation with low performance is also noteworthy.

Figure 7. **Mobile and fixed network penetration**

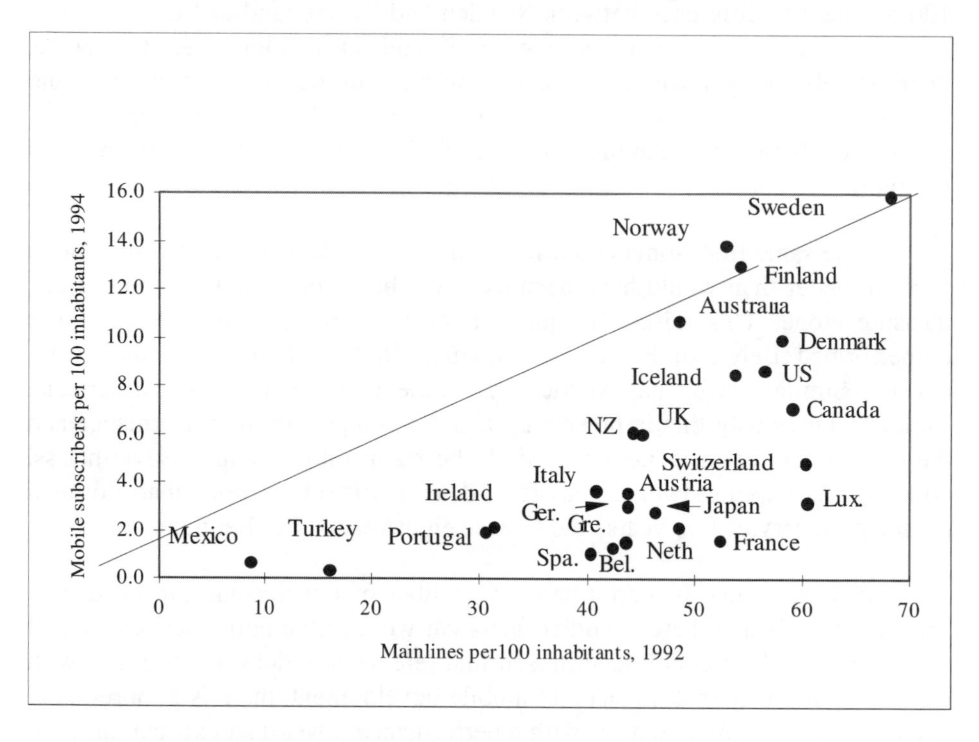

Market structure for the fixed network

A key factor in the development of mobile telecommunication is the regulation pertaining to the use of fixed networks. For competitors to an incumbent PTO, access to fixed networks is critically dependent on an appropriate interconnection regime and, where they deem it most efficient, the ability to use their own infrastructure. The lack of infrastructure competition in the PSTN in some countries is an acute problem for mobile operators because leased line prices are much higher on average than liberal markets. Moreover there is clearly a danger that incumbents can use their monopoly over leased line provision in anti-competitive ways, such as unnecessarily raising a competitor's costs, unreasonably delaying the provision of service or not ensuring a high quality of service for rivals.

Some problems posed by monopoly control of the PSTN can be effectively addressed by regulatory safeguards, such as monitoring quality of service and ensuring accounting separation to detect any attempt to cross subsidise competitive services from monopoly markets. In other cases regulators have decided that the problems raised by permitting monopoly PSTN operators to operate a service in competition with new players are such that it is better to initially structure the market so that there is a clear separation between different activities. For example BT was initially permitted to invest in Cellnet (the company holds a 60 per cent stake in the mobile operator) but not market services directly to customers. Like Vodafone, Cellnet had to market its products through service providers or subsidiaries. With additional operators in the fixed and mobile markets this restriction no longer applies. Similarly in Greece, OTE was not permitted to bid for the two initial licences granted to provide mobile telecommunication, ensuring a complete separation between wireless and PSTN networks while the two new wireless operators became established. OTE is now free to establish a service.

The best safeguards available are not a substitute for efficient infrastructure competition, and in practice can not address all anti-competitive behaviour by monopoly PSTN providers. A case has been reported in one Member country in which a PTO, which offered both PSTN and mobile services, offered corporate customers discounts on leased lines in return for transferring their mobile accounts from a competitor.[27] Such practices are very difficult to safeguard against, even with the most stringent regulation, and are undoubtedly beyond the resources available to enforce compliance. On the other hand infrastructure competition in the PSTN and a clear separation of the mobile operations from the PSTN are tools available to directly tackle attempts at anti-competitive behaviour.

The experience of France provides an example of where the first mobile competitor was initially prevented from investing in its own infrastructure for transmission.[28] This meant SFR had to rely on France Telecom, its competitor, to provide leased lines. This policy was reversed on 1 January 1994, when SFR was permitted to construct its own infrastructure. Worthy of note is that the number of new connections in 1994 was four times what it had been in 1992. The experience of Greece is also interesting because both mobile operators are independent from the PSTN operator and there is no incentive for OTE to favour or retard either STET or Panafon.

In many other EU countries, mobile operators must use leased lines from the fixed network operator. In Germany, Mannesmann and E-Plus, the two competitors to Deutsche Telecom can use their own microwave infrastructure to link base stations to switches but must still lease lines from Deutsche Telecom to transport traffic between switches.[29] Only in Finland, Sweden and the United Kingdom can mobile operators currently use their own infrastructure or have a choice of fixed line operators in the EU area.[30] Similarly in Mexico the regional mobile companies that compete with Telmex's subsidiary will not have a choice of long distance supplier until 1997. Those countries with a poorer national performance should pay careful attention to whether there is efficient interconnection between independent mobile operators and the PSTN.

The difference in performance between countries with seamless infrastructure competition and monopoly control of the fixed network is readily apparent. Figure 8 plots growth in 1994 against an index of liberalisation in which countries were awarded 2 points for permitting infrastructure competition in the PSTN (local and national) and mobile communication. It is demonstrable that mobile telecommunication markets are growing much faster in countries such as Australia, Finland, New Zealand, Japan, Sweden, the United Kingdom and United States where mobile operators enjoy a choice of fixed network operators than in monopoly markets.

Figure 8. **Mobile growth and infrastructure competition**

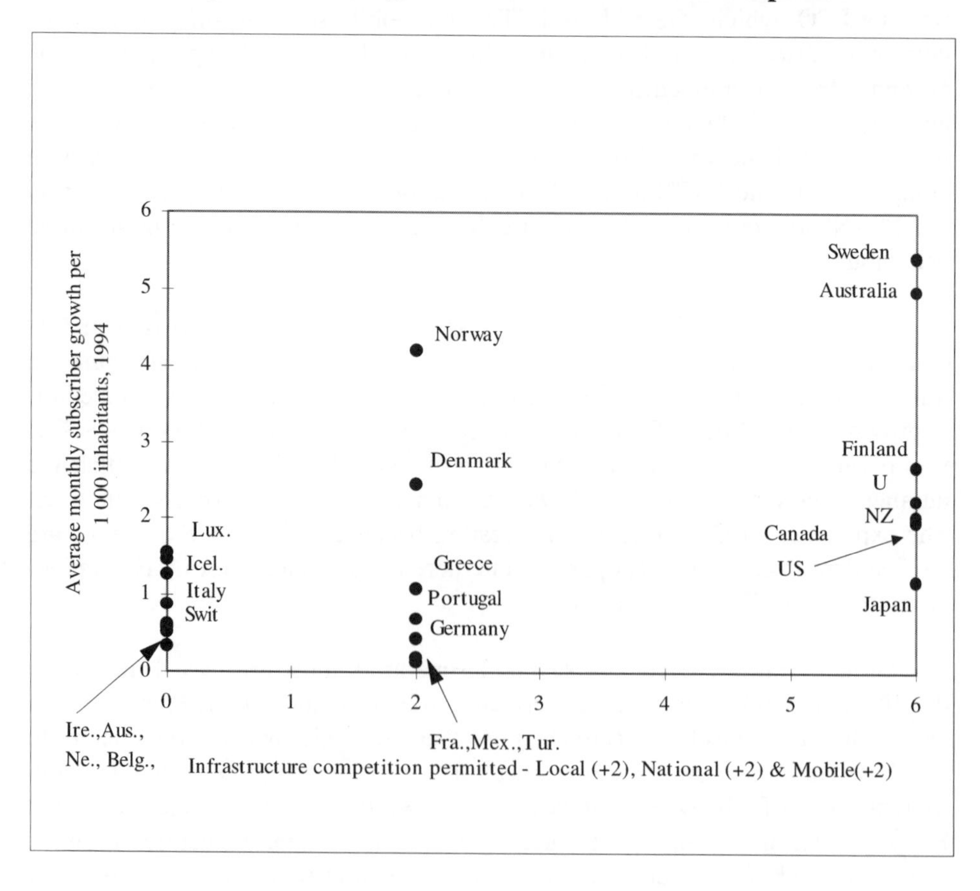

Separation of fixed and mobile operations

Given the problems regulators may encounter where there is bottleneck control over the PSTN with even the best safeguards, it has been decided in some countries to structure the market so that there is a clear distinction between fixed network and mobile operations. It has already been noted that there tends to be a correlation between good performance and the effective working of the market, either by insulating mobile market from possible anti-competitive practices by PSTN operators or more positively allowing infrastructure competition. On the other hand, from the perspective of PTOs there is growing evidence that separation of mobile and fixed operations has proven to be the most efficient way to develop mobile services. The available evidence continues to show that best practice in the provision of mobile telecommunication in the OECD area, in countries such as Sweden and Norway, is provided by independent subsidiaries and spin-off companies.

It is not surprising then that the first company to see the wisdom of independence for mobile operations was Telia, the company with the longest history in a competitive mobile market. In 1993 Telia's Radio Division was converted into a limited liability company, Telia Mobitel AB, but the process had begun long before this date. Writing on the history of mobile telephony in Nordic countries, Ove Granstrand has noted that Comvik's entry into the market in 1981 while not large in itself was very significant for Telia and brought with it recognition of the importance of a focused response:

> "Comvik contributed to the competitiveness of Televerket (now Telia) through indirectly spurring its competitive spirit, training it for competition, speeding up its investment in the network, etc. Marketwise Comvik never was really important in the 'NMT era' but culture-wise it was for Televerket Radio. It provided a threat (especially if a big foreign competitor acquired Comvik) and thus functioned in fact as a contestant with suitable size and power for Televerket Radio, which really was in a similar position as an infant industry both in terms of size and in terms of competitive experience. Televerket Radio became a precursor within Televerket regarding competition and market orientation. Televerket Radio also became a fairly independent subsidiary within Televerket...".[31]

Some PTOs have restructured their operations in the knowledge that they will have greater freedom from regulation to compete efficiently with other service providers. When Pacific Telesis spun-off its wireless operations to form AirTouch Communications, it noted that an important benefit of the plan was the freedom from line-of-business restrictions. These restrictions were imposed on the Regional Bell Operating Companies after the divestiture of AT&T to safeguard against anti-competitive practices resulting from bottleneck control of the PSTN. In 1993 Pacific Telesis noted,

> "... the separation would reduce the time and expense required to comply with rules that govern transactions between Bell operating companies and non-Bell affiliate companies. Freed from the 1982 Consent Decree, the spin-off company can provide long distance service without lengthy approvals, work closely with equipment companies to develop new technology and differentiate products, and enter new markets more freely."[32]

Yet while separation has advantages for both operators and governments in the form of 'lighter regulation', the primary reason for the spin-off of mobile operations are commercial. The main reasons given for the spin off of AirTouch was the flexibility it gave the new company to raise capital, both to finance the rapid expansion of service in 'home markets' and to bid for off-shore licences. Moreover in an increasingly competitive market, smaller spin-off companies, or highly independent subsidiaries, are able to adapt more quickly than PTOs with business cultures deriving from monopoly markets. This is one reason that Norwegian Telecom, one of the most successful operators of mobile services spun-off an independent subsidiary 'Tele-mobil' at the beginning of 1993. The company noted at that time that it wanted the new subsidiary to be run according to business principles in a competitive market. Similarly Telecom Italia is to spin-off its wireless operations in July 1995 as it faces competition for the first time.

Relative wealth of population

In respect to fixed network development analysts have often commented on the fairly close correlation between national wealth (GDP per capita) and the level of tele-density. Accordingly there are some similarities between Figures 7 and 9 in terms of country positions on the X-axis. Nevertheless, if a positive relationship exists, the question is raised as to why the three countries with the highest GDP per capita, Japan, Luxembourg and Switzerland, all have relatively low penetration rates. Of course there is a correlation between good performance and relatively high GDP per capita in Sweden, Norway and Finland but seemingly no more important than numerous other factors with which there is a correlation. The answer would appear to be that, while the relative wealth of a country can play a role in differences between development in OECD countries, it is subordinate to the efficiency of market structure.

This is exemplified in the significant differences between the performance of countries with similar levels of GDP per capita. Why, for instance, are New Zealand and Canada respectively outperforming Ireland and the Netherlands? The question is magnified when countries such as Australia and the United Kingdom, with lower GDP per capita, have been able to outperform many countries with much higher levels of GDP per capita such as Austria, Belgium and Italy. These differences in expected performance based on relative wealth have led analysts to also look at the pricing of services and growth rates.

Figure 9. **Mobile subscriber penetration and GDP**

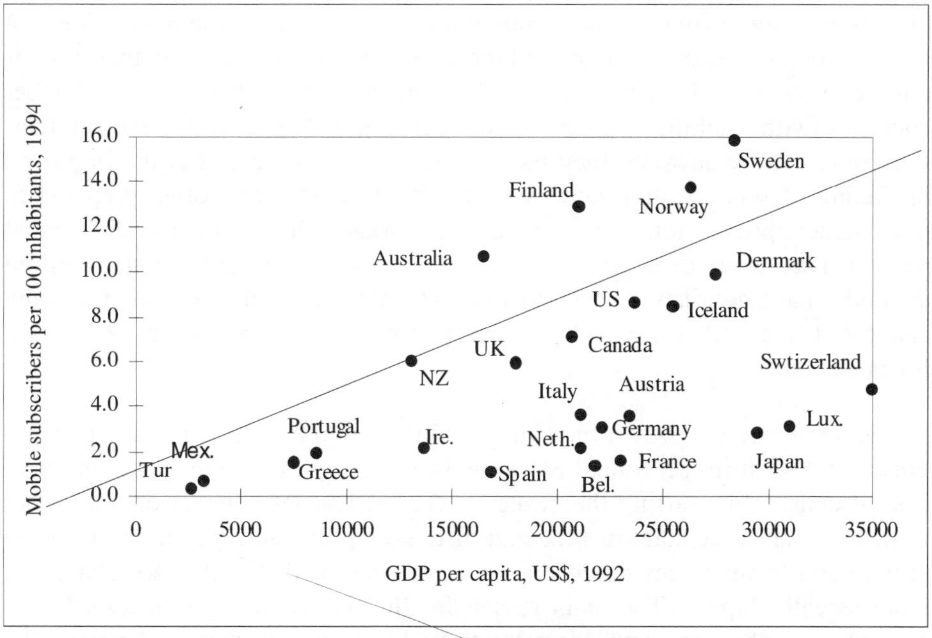

Price of service, revenue contribution and penetration

The cost of a basket of mobile telecommunication services varies greatly in the OECD (Table 10). Some have noted a correlation between the pricing of service and penetration rates (*i.e.* low prices and high penetration rates/high prices and low penetration rates).[33] Certainly those countries with low basket prices, such as the Scandinavian countries, tend to have high mobile telecommunication penetration rates. Yet some countries with relatively high penetration rates, and strong growth rates, also have above average prices for a basket of mobile services (New Zealand, the United Kingdom and the United States). Sometimes this is due to 'affordability'. For example, analysis of relative wealth and prices together (basket price as a per cent of GDP per capita) show that mobile telecommunication is more affordable in the United States than Ireland, even though prices are higher in the United States.

However using an 'affordability' approach to explaining performance tends to raise more questions than it answers. Why for example does New Zealand's rate of growth exceed Switzerland by three times even though its basket price as a percentage of GDP per capita is four times higher? Indeed, how did Portugal manage a growth rate comparable to Switzerland with a basket that cost eight times more as a percentage of GDP per capita? There are several reasons for these seeming anomalies. One reason is that the OECD mobile basket is built on the usage pattern of a business user, with standard price packages aimed at high users, rather than a personal communication user. Also the basket does not include volume discounts aimed at high users. A second reason is that price is only one aspect of marketing a telecommunication service, and Member countries with multiple operators have proven better able to expand their subscriber base even when they have higher prices. Indeed it is the improved marketing of services and increased attention to customers (often prepared to pay higher prices for the service they want) that explains differential performance rather than price. On the other hand it is notable that several duopolies have not distinguished themselves on price, such as France, Germany and the United States, which is one reason policy makers are increasing liberalisation.

In France the high cost of joining mobile networks seems to have retarded growth although in the United States and to a lessor extent Germany, the high cost of calls, while raising the basket price, has had less impact on subscriber growth. In all three countries the end of the duopoly can be expected to boost growth and lower prices based on the experience of the United Kingdom and more recently Japan. The main reason for this is that an open market forces operators to set prices, and differentiate tariffs, in a way that will expand the subscriber base beyond the business market. From a different perspective investment analysts have noted this trend in the United Kingdom which previously had prices as high as France, Germany and the United States and profit margins in excess of 40 per cent. In the context of historically "low" United Kingdom margins (36 per cent) one United Kingdom investment house has noted,

> "...there is significant risk that margins will not recover when growth slows. Any unanticipated deceleration in subscriber growth

can be expected to increase the intensity of competition (as individual players struggle to hit budgeted targets), and, in these conditions, falling numbers of new subscribers and connection bonuses may be offset by increasing per subscriber payments or price cuts ... Recent subscriber data has provided evidence of increased dependence on the personal sector for fuelling subscriber growth. Because these customers make little use of the network and have very low ongoing marginal costs they are currently profitable (although less profitable than business customers). Over the longer term, it is expected that monthly rentals for these customers will decrease significantly, and this gives rise to an additional concern over margins."[34]

From the perspective of policy makers, market structures that discipline prices and force incumbent operators (monopoly and duopoly) to look beyond any attempt to 'cream skim' the business market (by ignoring the less profitable personal communication market) are very welcome. In October 1994, analysis from another investment house concluded that the introduction of a third operator (E-Plus) would bring a profoundly different business strategy to the German market,

> "The target market which E-Plus will initially pursue (after extensive market testing) is small and medium businesses and consumers (for the first time), using an image as the 'friendly network' (as opposed to D1 and D2 who have to date marketed themselves at the top end of the market)... Moreover, E-Plus launched new low packages: 'Profi' for heavy users and 'Partner' for light users. D1 and D2 currently have only one set of tariffs each".[35]

With the onset of new operators, the nature of the mobile telecommunication business will change, and although the initially spectacular profit margins will be eroded by competition this will be offset by lower unit costs as the market expands (toward the OECD average of operating income before tax of 14 per cent of turnover). As might be expected, higher mobile telecommunication penetration rates are already enabling larger contributions to total telecommunication revenue. By 1992, countries such as Finland, Iceland, Norway and Sweden with high penetration rates had among the largest contributions to total telecommunication revenue from mobile telecommunication (Figure 10). In the United States mobile communication revenue is expected to make up 12 per cent of total telecommunication revenues by the end of 1995. In 1991 it had been just 4 per cent (Table 11).

Japan had a higher relative ratio of mobile revenue to total telecommunication revenue because the terminal market was not liberalised until April 1994. As mobile terminals had to be rented from operators in 1992, this boosted their mobile revenue rather than simply showing up in the sales of equipment vendors. The United Kingdom also had a higher relative contribution than might otherwise have been expected. Several factors may be at work here including the fact that some of Vodafone's offshore revenue would be included, albeit this was relatively small by 1992. In addition under the duopoly regime that existed during 1992, subscribers had to pay relatively high charges in the United Kingdom and Japan.

In 1992 there was a direct correlation between an OECD country's relative position of mobile revenue contribution/subscriber penetration ratio to the cost of a basket of mobile services. Countries below the line generally had relatively inexpensive mobile communication service baskets and those countries above the line had relatively expensive baskets. Exceptions were Finland, just above the line but relatively inexpensive, and New Zealand, just below the line with close to average charges for OECD countries in 1992. The least expensive seven countries for a basket of mobile services in 1992 were: **1.** Iceland, **2.** Denmark, **3.** Switzerland, **4.** Finland, **5.** Norway, **6.** Sweden, **7.** Canada. All these countries had relatively inexpensive baskets which coincided with higher mobile penetration rates. By way of contrast, most countries above the line generally had much higher relative charges for a basket of services.

Figure 10. **Mobile pentration and revenue contribution, selected OECD countries, 1992**

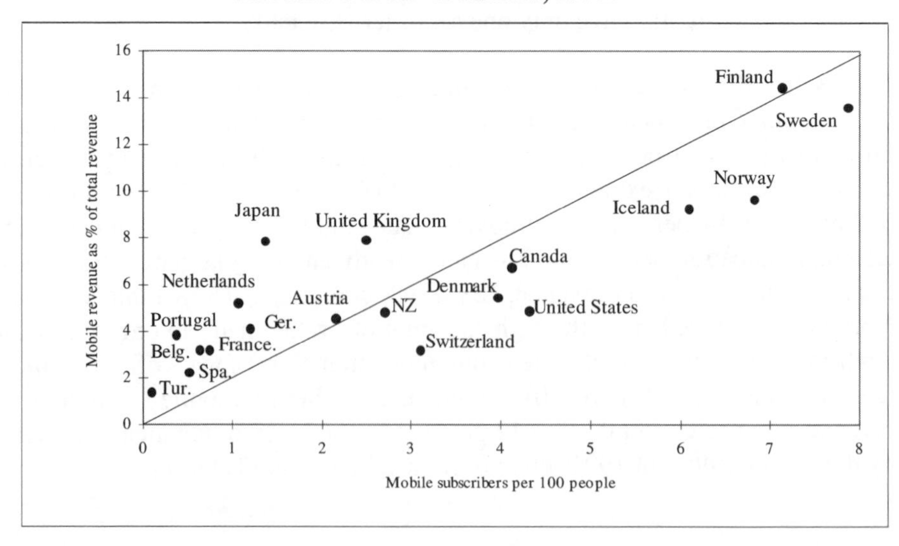

Table 10. OECD basket of analogue mobile telecommunication tariffs, January 1995

	Fixed Charge (US$ PPP)	Usage Charge (US$ PPP)	Total (US$ PPP)	Basket price as per cent of GDP per capita	Average monthly subs. per 1 000 inhabitants (1994)
Iceland	97.97	364.22	462.19	1.81	1.47
Denmark	108.86	546.35	655.21	2.38	2.44
Switzerland	372.46	562.04	934.50	2.67	0.88
Finland	105.35	499.50	604.85	2.88	2.68
Norway	176.98	629.37	806.35	3.06	4.19
Sweden	152.63	744.62	897.25	3.16	5.40
Canada	383.52	562.52	946.04	4.56	1.97
Netherlands	295.88	690.85	986.73	4.67	0.57
Luxembourg	626.57	972.33	1 598.90	5.15	1.53
Austria	385.71	845.18	1 230.89	5.26	0.60
Japan	630.02	1 019.21	1 649.23	5.59	1.18
Italy	435.23	755.53	1 190.76	5.62	1.50
Belgium	412.87	834.64	1 247.51	5.71	0.51
Australia	319.85	706.97	1 026.82	6.21	4.96
Germany	385.62	1 163.92	1 549.54	6.98	0.68
United Kingdom	496.34	868.57	1 364.91	7.55	2.25
United States	496.07	1 308.88	1 804.15	7.62	1.96
Ireland	390.07	720.91	1 110.98	8.10	0.62
France	929.56	1 046.70	1 976.26	8.58	0.43
Spain	523.81	966.47	1 490.28	8.84	0.33
New Zealand	534.22	931.37	1 465.59	11.18	2.04
Portugal	606.11	1 186.83	1 792.94	20.94	0.61
Mexico	386.84	1 533.65	1 920.49	58.91	0.17
Turkey	228.23	1 538.62	1 766.85	67.10	0.13
OECD	395.84	846.36	1 241.68	5.98	1.63

1. Greece is excluded because it does not have a comparable analogue service.
2. Average excludes Mexico and Greece.
3. There are 767 calls in the basket. Excluding tax.
4. Data for Germany, Iceland and Spain is for 1994.
5. 1992 GDP per capita data used.
6. Average monthly growth is a simple average for OECD.
7. Data for Canada is for a one cellular service provider. The results may vary with the tariffs of another mobile communications operator.

Source: OECD.

Table 11. **Actual and projected mobile network services revenue in the United States**
(US$ billion)

	1991	1992	1993	1994	1995	CAGR (per cent)
Network access	29.2	29.3	30.2	30.6	31.5	1.9
Long distance	39.5	41.7	43.8	46.0	83.7	5.6
Local service	39.5	41.7	43.8	46.0	48.2	5.1
Cellular and radio telephone	6.6	8.9	12.6	17.6	23.8	37.8
Directory advertising and other	17.1	17.9	18.8	19.5	20.5	4.6
Total	159.6	165.2	180.3	193.0	207.7	6.8

Source: NATA, Census Bureau, Annual Reports, CTIA, Telecommunications Reports.

The date of adoption

While higher penetration rates in some countries are because of an earlier service launch and greater network coverage of potential subscribers, this factor is diminishing in importance for comparisons of current growth rates. By 1992, most Member countries were reporting population coverage in excess of 80 per cent. More than 10 countries had coverage of more than 90 per cent of their population.[36] In fact population coverage can be achieved in fairly short time periods. In Germany Mannesmann Mobilfunk commenced commercial operations in June 1992 and by the end of 1994 covered approximately 94 per cent of the population, including all major cities and highways.[37] Similarly Telecel was awarded a licence by Portugal in October 1991 and commenced service in October 1992 covering all major cities and highways. By the end of 1994 Telecel had covered approximately 94 per cent of the population.[38] As an aside regulators have often placed obligations on licensees in terms of population coverage but increasingly the capacity of mobile networks, in terms of the quality of service it enables, will be a critical indicator of performance.

One reason for the increasingly rapid roll-out of service is technological change. In 1995 one manufacturer reported the development of a technology that will cut the number of PCS base stations needed in low traffic regions by 60 per cent. This enables networks to be planned and rolled out more rapidly and at lower cost.[39] In the context of the introduction of digital service in Germany it has been noted,

> "...many of the original GSM base stations were installed when the technology was in its infancy (1992) and hence both D1 and D2 originally deployed more expensive and cumbersome equipment than

is currently available (the physical size of the base stations often meant that installation was a civil engineering project). Now the base stations are sufficiently small to allow installation on roof tops. Thus with a key element of the cost of building a mobile network being site acquisition for base stations, the latest generation of much smaller base stations can be installed much more cheaply and effectively and indeed are more 'light' in terms of their effect on the skyline...E-Plus is realistically likely... to achieve 98 per cent coverage of the population (80 per cent geographic coverage) with approximately 5 800 cells (and using repeater technology in more rural areas which allows for coverage at one-third the cost of a base station)."[40]

At the same time comparisons of subscriber growth are inherently influenced by their starting point. Sometimes mobile telecommunication growth rates are spectacular simply because of a relatively low base number. While such comparisons are useful if they indicate an improvement in performance on a national basis, they tend to obscure relative performance gains in international comparisons.

Figure 11. **Competition and development**

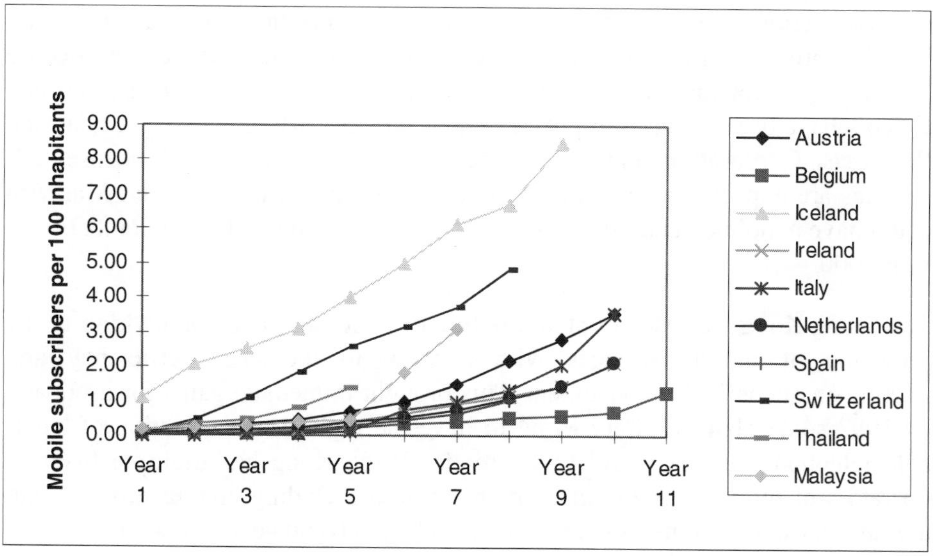

Box 6. Harnessing competition for development

Until relatively recently, with some notable exceptions, most OECD countries were proponents of state-owned monopolies providing telecommunication service. During the 1980s even the pioneers of liberalisation in mobile telecommunication were reluctant to go beyond two operators. The turning point came in 1992 when countries such as Australia, Sweden and the United Kingdom decided to go beyond duopolies. In this respect OECD countries were not leaders. Countries such as Thailand, Malaysia and Hong Kong had already decided that open competition was a tool that could be effectively applied to develop mobile telecommunication service. These three countries are particularly interesting because they share extremely positive results from liberalisation while having very diverse characteristics.

In 1990 Thailand took the initiative to allow multiple operators of analogue services (TOT, CAT, TAC and AIS).[41] In a liberal market environment Thailand's growth in mobile subscribers has outstripped many OECD countries (Figure 11). After five years of open competition Thailand was ahead of 15 OECD countries in subscriber penetration after equivalent time periods -- all of which had monopolies or duopolies. Malaysia has also introduced three analogue operators (Telkom Malaysia, Mobikom, and Celcom). The experience with competition has been in some respects even more successful than Thailand. This has prompted the Malaysian Government to take the next step and license five operators for digital services (Table 12). Two companies, Binariang and Celcom have been licensed to provide GSM services, while Berjaya, Malaysian Resources Corporation and Sapura have been awarded a PCS license. All services are expected to commence in 1995, and it is estimated that Malaysia could have a mobile penetration rate of 15 subscribers per 100 inhabitants by the year 2000.

Hong Kong has also adopted a policy of fostering open competition in the provision of mobile services with a view to increasing efficiency and maximising benefits for consumers. This brought immediate gains for users and by 1992 some claimed Hong Kong to have the highest concentration of hand-held telephones in the world.[42] Currently, Hong Kong has multiple licensed operators of mobile telecommunication services including analogue, CT-2 and digital services. Some operators have taken advantage of new licences to migrate services to a digital environment. While the market is reportedly already very competitive, Hong Kong proposes to award six licences for PCS services.

Several analysts have tried to pinpoint reasons for the success of mobile telecommunication in Hong Kong, Malaysia and Thailand. For example, it is posited that the low penetration rate of fixed telephone lines in Thailand has been a primary factor in the growth of the mobile market. While Thailand's low fixed-line penetration has no doubt been an ingredient in the rapid build up of mobile services, this raises the question of why developing countries with similar rates of fixed-line penetration have not had the same success? More fundamentally, why have rapid growth rates been experienced in Hong Kong and Malaysia, given that they have much higher telecommunication penetration rates? In short, there is demand for mobile telecommunication irrespective of a country's fixed-line penetration if it can be efficiently met. Hong Kong has a fixed-line penetration rate higher than the OECD average and uncharged local calls! The difference between the success of these three countries, and others, is more likely due to market liberalisation.

Table 12. **Leading applications of competition outside the OECD area**

	Hong Kong	Malaysia	Thailand
Mobile subscribers, 1994 (000)	424.9 (analogue) N.A. (C-T2) N.A. (digital)	615.0	781.0
Subs. per 100 inhabitants, 1994 (1)	7.3+	3.1	1.4
Mainlines per 100 inhabitants, 1992	48.6	11.1	3.1
Population, 1992 (m)	5.8	18.8	57.8
GDP per capita, 1991 (US$)	14 155	2 545	1 640
Analogue operators	Huchinson HKT - CSL Pacific Link Chevalier (CT-2)	Telekom Malaysia Mobikom Celcom	TOT CAT AIS TAC
GSM digital operators and launch date	HKT- CSL, 1993 SmarTone Mobile Comms, 1993 Huchinson, 1995	Binariang, 1995 Celcom, 1995	AIS, 1994
PCS digital operators and launch date	Six proposed DCS 1800 licences to be awarded.	Berjaya, 1995 Malaysia Resources Corp, 1995 Sapura, 1995 (2)	TAC, 1994

1. Mid-1994 data used for Hong Kong and Thailand.
2. Mutiara Telecommunications has also been licensed to provide PCS services bringing the total number of licences to eight.

Source: OECD, ITU, APEC, Mobile Communications International, Datapro.

DEVELOPMENTS IN MOBILE PRICING

Tariff trends

The basic components of mobile telecommunication tariffs mirror the PSTN. Essentially, there are 'fixed' charges (connection and subscription tariffs) and 'usage' charges (price of calls). The term tariff structure refers to the balance between fixed and usage charges in the pricing of telecommunication services. Over the past decade there has been a general trend toward rebalancing PSTN tariffs by maintaining or increasing fixed charges while lowering usage charges over longer distances. In mobile communication the reverse has been true as operators seek to bring down entry costs. In the OECD basket for mobile telecommunication, the average price of fixed charges (yearly rental and connection cost divided by three) has been decreasing faster than average call charges. In 1989 the average fixed component of the OECD mobile telephone basket was US$564 based on purchasing power parity (PPP) compared to US$396 by 1995 (Figure 12). This represented a 30 per cent reduction. The average call charge in the OECD basket hase also decreased since 1989 from US$1.35 to US$1.10 expressed in PPPs, an 18 per cent reduction.[43]

Figure 12. **Mobile communication price trends in the OECD**

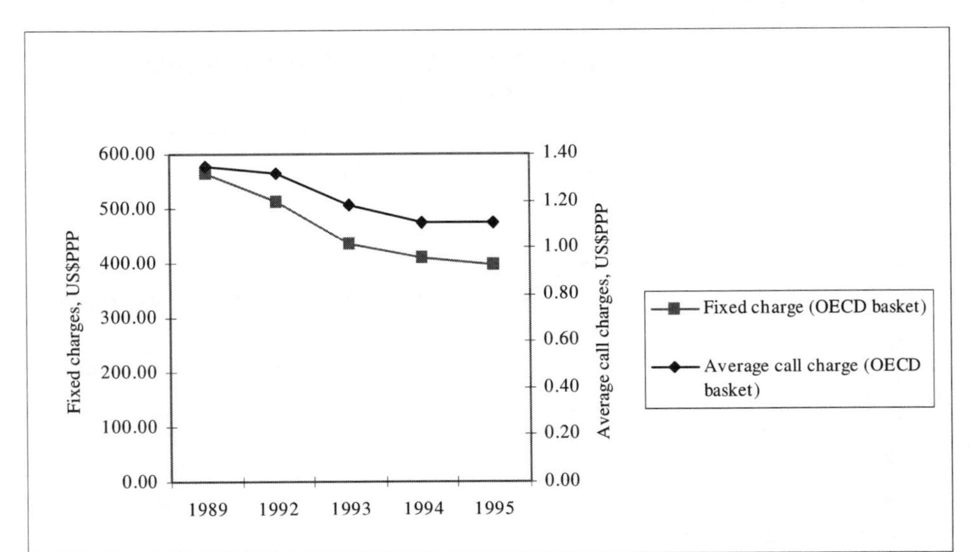

In terms of price (rather than cost - see discussion below) mobile telecommunication is still much more expensive than the fixed network. The average cost of a call for a user in the OECD business basket for the PSTN is US$0.27, nearly four times less expensive than an average mobile call. The average fixed charge for a telecommunication mainline to a business premise (US$181) is less than half that of the average mobile telecommunication fixed charge. Much of the reason fixed charges are falling faster than call charges is the growing competition for market share. This trend does not always appear in analysis of standard published tariffs. For example in the United Kingdom usage charges have fallen since the abolition of the duopoly (notably because of the abolition of a surcharge for calls in the London area) much faster than fixed charges (Figure 13). However in many cases operators are willing to waive connection fees for new customers.

In respect to the G-7 countries, there have been significant price reductions in Germany, Japan and the United Kingdom (Figure 14). Prices in the other G-7 countries have remained fairly constant since 1992 illustrating that the strong growth in Canada and the United States, and to lessor extent Italy, has been more the result of price differentiation than reduction. This is not to argue that price reductions are not enough to stimulate growth, but rather that a combination of lower prices and tariff differentiation have driven the market in countries such as the United Kingdom. For users in Canada, different pricing packages are built on an already low price regime, whereas in France the new range of tariffs, while increasing subscriber numbers, had not had the same impact because of a high price regime.

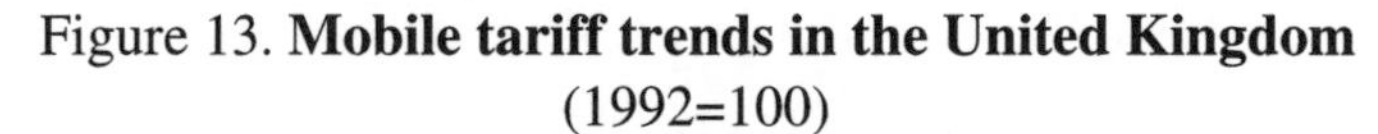

Figure 13. **Mobile tariff trends in the United Kingdom**
(1992=100)

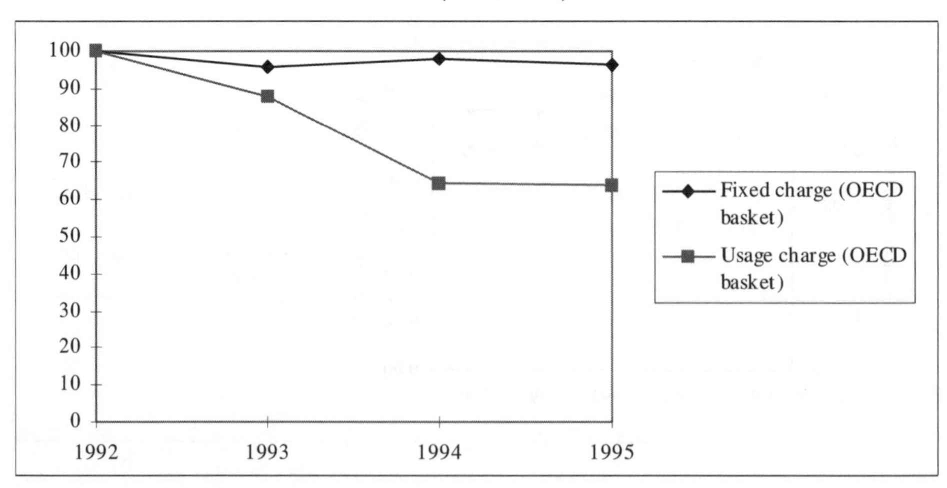

Figure 14. **Mobile communication OECD basket trends**
(G7 countries)

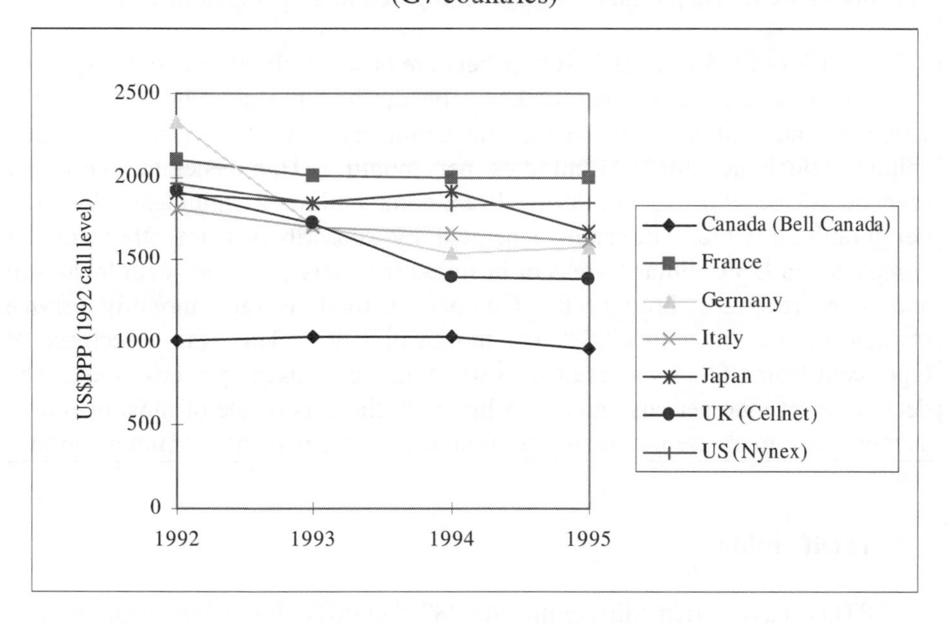

Box 7. Profiling Mobile telecommunication users: United States Cellular Corporation

The United States Cellular Corporation (US Cellular) is the seventh largest cellular telecommunication company in the United States, based on the population coverage of areas it owns or has the right to acquire.[44] The Company acquires, manages, owns, operates and invests in cellular systems throughout the United States. As of December 31 1993, the Company owned or had the right to acquire interests in Metropolitan Statistical Areas ("MSAs") and Rural Service Areas ("RSAs") with an aggregate population of approximately 23.7 million in a total of 205 markets.[45]

To date the main use of the Company's mobile telecommunication services has been by business users. Data for 1993 indicate that 52 per cent of customers use their cellular telephones primarily for business. US Cellular reports its subscribers come from a wide range of occupations including a large proportion of people who work outside of their offices in fields such as construction, real estate, wholesale and retail distribution businesses, and professionals. At the end of 1993 most customers still used cellular telephones installed in their vehicles. However, the balance between 'car telephones' and hand-held terminals is changing. In 1993, 71 per cent of customers joining US Cellular's network chose to use portable handsets compared to 21 per cent in 1988.

As most of US Cellular's subscribers are business users, it is not surprising the networks are used most extensively during 'business hours' between 7:00 a.m. and 6:00 p.m. On average, the Company's own subscribers used their cellular telephones for 103 minutes per month. This generated customer revenue of US$49 per month during 1993, compared to 121 minutes and US$52 per month in 1992. Revenue generated by subscribers from other cellular companies in US Cellular's areas of business (roamers), together with local, toll and other revenues, brought the Company's total average monthly service revenue per customer to US$99 per month in 1993. This was a decrease of 6 per cent from 1992 as a result of lower volume of usage per customer. The decline in revenue per customer is in line with the experience of most operators as more customers use mobile telecommunication for personal communication.

Tariff options

PTOs have often differentiated PSTN tariffs for fixed charges and occasionally even usage charges. In respect to fixed charges the main difference has been charging different rates for business and residential users. Originally price discrimination was used as a tool to ration service to those most able to afford higher prices and garner capital to expand the network. Business was prepared to pay higher charges because they could get service faster and the charges were generally tax deductible. On the other hand it has been rare for PTOs to vary usage charges. In other words both business and residential users paid the same charges to make a call. There was price discrimination, in the sense that peak rates applied to business hours and discounts were usually available during 'non business hours' when most residential calls are made, but this pricing structure was as much about making efficient use of networks as about marketing.

In the first decade of mobile telecommunication most operators offered only one tariff structure. In other words they only offered the equivalent of a 'business tariff' option on the fixed network. Perhaps the major difference between the pricing of mobile communication and the PSTN in some countries was that operators charged both the originator and the recipient of the call at the same time. In addition many operators have a uniform tariff for national calls, which is independent of distance, rather than price bands that characterise long distance calls on the PSTN. More recently the pricing of mobile communication has radically departed from the PSTN model with differentiation between users for both fixed and usage charges. Indeed in the new environment of mobile pricing, the range of prices a user may pay for the same service is dramatically increasing. For example the same call on BC Tel Mobility's network, a Canadian operator, may be charged at one of six different rates (Free, C$ 0.20, C$ 0.25, C$ 0.35, C$ 0.55, C$ 0.95) depending on the time of day/week, call to designated location (*i.e.* home), and the amount of fixed charge paid (of which there are eight different rates for monthly charges). Moreover, while some tariff options mirror rebalancing on the PSTN (or more accurately exaggerate), others are in complete contrast. Several tariff strategies for 'non-business users' have dramatically lowered fixed charges and raised call charges; the reverse of many PTO's rebalancing on the fixed network.

These new tariff packages are designed to attract personal communication users but not to encourage the total migration of business users from the initial tariff options. In this sense the new tariff schemes represent the first stage of a competitive market with operators seeking to differentiate their products by pricing options rather than competing directly on price. This strategy is optimal from the point of view of mobile operators because the market is rapidly expanding, due in large part to the availability of these options, lessening the necessity to compete on price. As competition increases it would be expected that operators would compete more on price. In the more advanced tariff strategies discounts are increasingly available for the most lucrative customers but increased competition should also lower standard prices in future. For example, in the case of BC Tel Mobility, the above tariffs, for the fixed and usage components of service, are subject to volume discounts, meaning that the actual range of prices paid by different users is greater again. It is instructive to examine these strategies in more detail.

Low user schemes (raising usage and lowering fixed charges)

To date, one of the most successful tariff strategies adopted by operators has been to change the balance between fixed and usage charges by raising call charges and lowering fixed charges. One example is provided by Cellnet in the United Kingdom (Table 13). The aim of such an option is to attract users with a lower connection and rental charge (*e.g.* 'Cellnet Lifetime') than a standard pricing package (*e.g.* 'Cellnet Primetime'). For users who value the convenience and security of mobile communication, and who can achieve these goals with a limited number of calls, 'low user schemes' can offer tremendous advantages over standard pricing packages.

Table 13. **Cellnet standard and low user tariff options in the United Kingdom**

	Connection charge	Monthly rental	Peak rate per minute	Off-peak rate per minute	1/2 minute billing after the first minute
Cellnet Primetime,(£)	58.75	29.38	0.29	0.29	0.12
Cellnet Lifetime,(£)	29.38	15.00	0.50	0.50	0.20

Source: Cellnet.

Airtime options (raising fixed and lowering usage charges)

Another approach to tariffication has been pioneered by Orange, a PCS provider in the United Kingdom, by including airtime charges in the fixed component (Table 14). The advantage of this option is that users who make a lot of calls at peak times are able to reduce their bills by buying airtime in advance of use at lower rates. Orange recommends users who make 70 per cent of their calls at peak times and 30 per cent at off-peak times to use the following options 'talk 15' (0-70 minutes per month); 'talk 60' (71-225 minutes per month); 'talk 200' (226-380 minutes per month); 'talk 360' (381-565 minutes per month); 'talk 540' (more than 565 minutes per month).

Table 14. **Orange pricing plans in the United Kingdom, November 1994**

Plan name	Monthly charge (£)	Airtime included in monthly charge (minutes)	Standard call charges (per minute) peak & off-peak (£)		Orange to Orange call charges (per minute) (£)
Talk 15	15.00	15	0.25	0.125	0.125
Talk 60	25.00	60	0.20	0.10	0.10
Talk 200	50.00	200	0.18	0.90	0.90
Talk 360	75.00	360	0.16	0.80	0.80
Talk 540	100.00	540	0.14	0.70	0.70

Source: Orange.

Discount schemes

Mobile operators have developed several types of discount schemes to attract heavy users of services. For example Orange offers a discount of £5 on each of its pricing plans shown in Table 14 to customers with a second subscription. Discounts are not only available on fixed charges. Optus Communications in Australia offers customers discount on call charges once they have exceeded prepaid airtime amounts (Table 15). For example a subscriber to the Optus 'Business plan' would receive a 10 per cent discount on all calls billed over US$20. This discount builds to 20 per cent on all calls billed over US$40. In addition, Optus offers discounts on customer bills when the amounts exceed their fixed airtime plans (*i.e.* 'PowerPlan 120' and 'PowerPlan 240'). Another example of a discount scheme aimed at business users is provided by Cellular One in the United States (Table 16). For business users with between five and 24 mobile subscriptions, and more than 25 mobile subscriptions, volume discounts are available on call charges. Users also have the option of paying a higher rental in return for free off-peak calls between 8 p.m. and 7 a.m. from Monday to Friday, and all day on weekends.

Table 15. **Optus Communications pricing plan, October 1994**

	Monthly service charge (A$)	Includes call value of (A$)	Call charges (per 30 seconds) (A$)				Discount on call charges
			Local peak	Long distance peak	Local off-peak	Long distance off-peak	
Business Plan	35		0.20	0.30	0.10	0.15	10 per cent after A$20 of calls 20 per cent after A$40 of calls
Security Plan	20		0.40	0.60	0.10	0.15	
Freedom Plan	10		0.60	0.90	0.10	0.15	
PowerPlan 120	120	110	0.20	0.30	0.10	0.15¢	20 per cent after $110 of calls
PowerPlan 240	210	280	0.20	0.30	0.10	0.15¢	20 per cent after $280 of calls

Source: Optus Communications.

Table 16. **Cellular One Pricing Plans (Volume Discounts)**

	5-24 mobile subscriptions(US$)			25+ mobile subscriptions(US$)		
Monthly access fee	15.00		38.95	15.00		34.95
minutes	Prime(1)	Non-prime	Non-prime	Prime	Non-prime	Non-prime
First 100	0.37	0.17	Free	0.35	0.17	Free
101-300	0.35	0.16	Free	0.33	0.16	Free
301-600	0.34	0.15	Free	0.32	0.15	Free
600+	0.33	0.14	Free	0.31	0.14	Free

1. Cellular One defines Prime time as being from 7 a.m. - 9 p.m., Monday - Friday. However for these packages a further discount is available in that prime time is defined as 7 a.m. - 8 p.m., Monday - Friday.

Source: Cellular One.

Customisation for different types of users

One of the advantages stemming from a competitive market is that operators are increasingly differentiating tariff packages to attract distinct types of users. Two good examples are provided from the tariff options on offer to the customers of Comviq in Sweden (Table 17) and BC Tel Mobility in Canada (Table 18). Comviq offers four packages, two of which are aimed at business users ('Bas' and 'Office'), and two at personal communication users ('Private' and 'Compis'). Both the 'business options' include volume discounts but the 'Office' package is distinguished by higher fixed charges. The reason for the higher charge is that the 'Bas' option is the mobile equivalent of the plain ordinary telephone service on the PSTN. This option would suit business customers mainly wanting to use mobile communication for voice services. With the 'Office' package users not only have access to a range of value added features such as call waiting, personal answering, call transferring, call blocking etc., but can connect their personal computers to the digital mobile network to send data and faxes.

In respect to personal communication users, Comviq offers a low users scheme ('Private') and an option that provides a low rental and free calls to other 'Compis' subscribers. The use of uncharged calls at particular times of day, or with certain subscribers and locations, is an increasingly common marketing tool in competitive markets. The technique, pioneered by mobile telecommunication operators such as One-2-One in the United Kingdom and BC Tel Mobility in Canada, has also been adopted by some Cable Communication companies in the United Kingdom market for local telecommunication services. BC Tel Mobility has eight tariff options aimed at different types of customers. These packages include those designed for very low users concerned with security ('Lifeline'), and schemes for high users with volume discounts (*e.g.* 'Preferred Pak 120'). Several BC Tel Mobility packages also make use of uncharged calls on weekends or to a particular destination (*i.e.* subscriber's home number).

Table 17. **Comviq pricing plans, 1995**

Name of option	"Bas"	"Office"	"Private"	"Compis"
Fixed charges(SEK)				
Connection	370	493	199	370
Rental (monthly)	119	219	0 or 125 (2)	50
Usage charges (SEK per minute)				
Monday-Saturday			Monday-Friday	
07.00-19.00	3.50	3.50	5.00	5.00
19.00-01.00	2.25	2.25	2.00	2.00
01.00-07.00	1.13	1.13	1.00	1.00
Sunday/Public holidays			Saturday-Sunday	
07.00-01.00	1.80	2.25	2.00	2.00
01.00-07.00	0.90	1.13	1.00	1.00
	These prices apply up to 140 minutes. A discount of 21 per cent applies between 141-450 minutes and 25 per cent above 451 minutes.			Free calls to other Compris subscribers between Monday - Friday 21.00 - 07.00 and weekends.

1. All charges include sales tax
2. If use exceeds 30 minutes there is no rental charge applicable.

Source: Comviq.

Table 18. **BC Tel Mobility mobile communication pricing packages**

Plan name(1)	Monthly rental (C$)	Minutes	Usage charge
Preferred Pak 120	89.95	0-120	Included.
		121-499	0.25
		500+	0.20
Preferred Pak 30	29.95	0-30	Included
		31-120	0.55
		121-480	0.35
		481+	0.25
Home Free	45.95	100 calls home	Free
		Weekends	Free
		Weekdays	0.55
Home Free Plus	69.95	100 calls home	Free
		Peak(2)	0.55
		Off-peak	Free
50/50 Pak	49.95	0-50	Included
		51+	0.55
		Weekends	Free
Equalizer Plan	35.95	Weekdays	0.55
		Weekends	Free
Basic Service	24.95	0-120	0.55
		121-480	0.35
		481+	0.25
Lifeline	9.95	All minutes	0.95

1. Volume discounts apply to the fixed monthly charge and usage charges as follows: 10 telephones (5 per cent); 25 telephones (7.5 per cent); 50 telephones (10 per cent); 75 telephones (12.5 per cent); 100 telephones (15 per cent).
2. Peak hours are weekdays between 7 a.m. - 8 p.m. Off-peak hours are weekdays between 8 p.m. - 7 a.m. and all day Saturday and Sunday.

Source: BC Tel Mobility.

Box 8. Mobile operator's strategies for growth

Most PTOs in the OECD area say they are moving their prices more into line with the cost of providing service. One of the reasons for this tariff restructuring is the increasingly competitive market faced by telecommunication operators. When a competitor targets a particular market, operators generally want their prices to closely reflect cost. If they do not, all else being equal, it would be expected that the PTO would quickly lose market share to a competitor. On the other hand if it can be shown that a PTO lowers prices below costs in a particular market, to meet the challenge of a more efficient supplier, they are generally held to be acting in an anti-competitive manner. In the field of telecommunication this may be a problem where incumbent operators still have reserved services or bottleneck control of access facilities from which they can potentially cross subsidise services in competitive markets. This caveat aside and with due safeguards, such as structural or accounting separation, it can be expected that competition will drive prices closer to costs.

By way of contrast, many mobile telecommunication companies, and in particular those in some of the most competitive markets, are actively cross subsidising sales handsets (including installation). This may seem paradoxical but the strategies are similar to those of many fixed network operators at similar stages of development. Historically many PTOs have not priced the cost of installation of a mainline to a customers premise at full cost, preferring to recoup the expense through higher usage charges and line rentals.[46] This is particularly true of mid-range telephone penetration rates when PTOs are looking to expand their subscriber base, or high penetration rates where there may be a policy to satisfy unmet demand for reasons of universal service. In the case of a very low penetration rate, as in many developing countries, the operator often charges above cost to raise capital and ration demand.

The development of mobile telecommunication is different in two respects from the PSTN. First, in most countries the roll-out of the fixed network was undertaken by a single operator. By way of contrast, most mobile operators today have to compete for customers. Second, the difference between the cost of building and operating a mobile network and current usage charges would appear to be very large. In other words operators reckon it to be more profitable in the long run to subsidise customers joining the network. One example of this strategy is provided by the actions of US Cellular. In 1993 the company's revenue from handsets and installation was U$127 per unit. However the cost to the company was US$309, so on each transaction the company lost US$182 (Table 19). As US Cellular explains,

> "The average revenue per unit decline partially reflects the Company's decision to reduce sales prices on cellular telephones to increase the number of customers, to maintain its market position and to meet competitive prices as well as to reflect reduced manufacturers' prices. Also, during the second half of 1993, the Company used specific promotions which were based on increased equipment discounting. The success of these promotions led to both an increase in units sold and a decrease in average equipment sales revenue per unit."[47]

In respect to below cost connections, the strategies of mobile telecommunication companies might be likened to those of cable communication companies in the United Kingdom. In the face of BT's installed base, cable companies sometimes offer free or below cost connections to attract customers away from the incumbent. The major difference for mobile operators, in markets where operators commenced service at the same time, is that penetration rates are usually similar. Here the challenge is to build market share as quickly as possible, particularly if more operators will be introduced in future. For policy makers the major issue associated with pricing connections and handsets below cost is to ensure that PSTN operators are not cross subsidising this activity from other areas of monopoly service. This activity alone presents a sound case for accounting separation between mobile and PSTN services.

Table 19. **Subsidising handset purchase (US Cellular)**

	1991	1992	1993
Total operating revenue	99 477 000	164 085 000	247 259 000
Total operating expenses	116 308 000	176 790 000	255 915 000
Equipment sales (revenue from handsets and installation)	7 500 000	9 263 000	10 510 000
Cost of equipment sales (cost of handsets and installation)	13 575 000	17 311 000	25 688 000
Loss on handset sales	(6 075 000)	(8 048 000)	(15 178 000)
Number cellular telephones sold	29 400	44 400	83 000
Revenue per handset	255	208	127
Cost of handset sale (including accessories and installation)	462	390	309
Loss per handset sale	(207)	(182)	(182)

Source: US Cellular Corporation.

NETWORK CONVERGENCE AND PRICING

Mobile and fixed networks: cost, competition and pricing

The issues raised by the convergence between mobile and fixed telecommunication networks, particularly questions on the complementary and competitive nature of different networks, were considered by ICCP in 1991.[48] It is not intended to repeat the work undertaken in OECD (1995) "Mobile and PSTN Communications Services: Competition or Complementarity" OCDE/GD(95)96, particularly the analysis relating to regulatory questions which remains extremely robust. However the wave of liberalisation that has occurred in the OECD area since that time, and as a result the beginning of a significant drive into the personal communication market from 1992, it is necessary to reconsider some aspects of the report in relation to pricing.

The report concluded that in those regions which have well developed mobile communication services (such as Scandinavia) there was already a degree of competition and substitution between mobile and the PSTN by 1991. The report further stated that the degree of competition and substitution could be expected to increase over time. Nevertheless, the report's analysis showed that the pricing of mobile communication networks was substantially higher than fixed networks. For example it was noted that the price of a basket of mobile telecommunication services was four times as expensive as a business basket for fixed services.[49] In 1992, the price differential between a basket of mobile services was six to eight times that of fixed services in the Netherlands and Germany. This analysis seemed to confirm the proposition that substantial competition between different types of networks was a fairly distant possibility. The fact that the price comparison was between mobile and business baskets, rather than residential baskets, lent further support to the contention that competition between mobile operators and fixed networks for non-business users was even more remote.

At the same time the report, in considering tariff comparisons between networks and countries, made reference to the fact that it was necessary to take underlying costs into account when it stated,

> "It is difficult to know whether or not this tariff structure[mobile communication] is truly cost based. On the one hand it is logical for the start-up costs for a mobile service to be much lower than the PSTN as it is not necessary to lay or maintain cables and therefore the operators fixed charges are lower."[50]

and

> "There is no obvious explanation for these large differences in pricing policy between countries and they reinforce the suspicion that mobile tariffs are rarely cost-based, despite the introduction of [duopoly] competition in some countries."[51]

Both these statements deserve further consideration for a number of reasons. First, the situation in 1995 is very different from 1991 in terms of the degree of market liberalisation and, as a result, the economics of mobile communication networks. In respect to market structure, by 1991 only a handful of OECD countries had introduced competition and no country had gone beyond a duopoly market structure. In those countries to introduce duopolies, one licence was either awarded directly to the operator(s) of the PSTN (Japan, Mexico, Sweden, the United States), or the fixed network operator(s) held a substantial share-holding in one of the two new licences (Canada, the United Kingdom). Accordingly, not only did incumbent operators not have an incentive to price mobile services to be competitive with the PSTN, they found they could charge a premium for the flexibility of mobile telecommunication. In the context of a duopoly the second operator took the prices of the incumbent as their reference, not the fixed network. As a more fully mature competitive market emerges, prices for substitutable communication services can be expected to converge.

Second, a focus on prices rather than cost, tends to understate the potential of mobile telecommunication to compete with fixed networks in the new regulatory environments. While it is true that mobile networks faced lower start-up costs than fixed networks, it has taken a decade for the average operating cost per customer to approach the average cost per mainline for the PSTN. For example, in the United Kingdom, Vodafone's average cost per customer is now lower than BT's average cost per mainline[52] (Table 20). Moreover this has been achieved at a time when considerable costs have been incurred by Vodafone in providing bonuses to service suppliers and rolling out its digital network.

The main reason for this trend, and the increased pace of its development, is the expansion of the subscriber base and the impact of competition on lowering costs. To an extent technological change is also lowering the average cost per subscriber but this is more influential in the economics of new networks. In fact the cost of technology is becoming less significant as a percentage of total costs in a more competitive environment, and the costs of mobile operators and PSTN operators are converging on the same areas. Ericsson, the leading manufacturer of mobile telecommunication equipment, has published the following perspective on current developments,

> "The real potential will come when penetrations exceed 10 per cent - a barrier many see as the threshold to the mass market. The mass market has become a fashionable target, regulatory and licensing procedures are now encouraging the cellular industry to tackle the consumer segment. But the mass market is still some way away - and will not arrive until terminal prices and tariffs are both reduced significantly. Most cellular operators to date have had little incentive to reduce tariffs. Even when they faced competition from other cellular operators, the business market was large enough to go round. During the 1980s, some industry observers even described a cellular licence as a licence to print money. In the 1990s, a few observers still see it that way - but with operators printing twenty dollar rather than hundred dollar bills.
>
> The trend is clear. Competition is getting fiercer, increasing the cost of acquiring new subscribers. And as penetration levels rise, the average value of each new subscriber decreases. These inevitable consequences of competition will be magnified over the next few years. The current tendency is to licence many more than two operators per area, up to eight in the case of PCS in the United States, forcing operators to look beyond the business market for subscribers. In such circumstances, the costs of acquiring and maintaining subscribers will far exceed the cost of equipment. A typical cellular operator will spend approximately 10 per cent of total expenditure on electronics, the rest going on items such as marketing, billing, real estate and interconnect charges."[53]

The latter charges detailed by Ericsson are in many respects the same as a fixed network operator, such as billing, and can be expected to reduce as economies develop from larger subscriber bases. Indeed four OECD countries, Sweden, Norway, Finland and Australia had exceeded 10 subscribers per 100 inhabitants by the end of 1994. However it is difficult to discern how far the trend can continue if the major areas of cost mirror those of the fixed network rather than being technology-based. In Sweden, the OECD country with the highest penetration rate and the longest history of service, Telia Mobile's operating cost per customer had decreased to US$426 after being US$668 in 1991 (Table 21). This was US$44 lower than the average operating cost per mainline, but PSTN costs per mainline are also being reduced. Interestingly Telia Mobile's cost per customer were still about double the price of a basket of residential services over the fixed network in 1994 (US$218 with 996 calls). Telia is one of the most efficient PSTN operators in the OECD and from a different perspective Telia Mobile's costs per customer are drawing near the OECD average basket price for residential users in 1994 (US$373 with 996 calls).

In the United States the cross-over point in terms of fixed and mobile average costs appears to have occurred at around the same time as in the United Kingdom and Sweden (Table 22). A comparison between a fixed network operator (Nynex) and a mobile operator (AirTouch) shows the average cost per mobile customer is already lower than the average cost per mainline. In Germany a comparison between a fixed network operator (Deutsche Telecom) and a specialist mobile operator (Mannesmann) shows the same trend and a cross-over should occur in the near future (Table 23). From a different perspective the average costs of the same company (BC Tel) in providing mobile telecommunication exhibit the same trend although in this case the cross-over point has not yet been reached (Table 24).

While comparisons between the average costs per mainline and per customer of fixed and mobile networks provide only one perspective on cost, all indications are that the economics of mobile communication are rapidly changing as the customer base expands. In the first decade of mobile telecommunication development the average cost per subscriber was greater than the average cost per mainline of the PSTN but this situation is now reversing. The key point for policy makers is that regulatory frameworks are available to take advantage of the changing costs in the provision of telecommunication service. The introduction of a second mobile operator is a good first step, but Member countries may find that where one of the duopolists is owned by the fixed network operator, benefits are slower to accrue.

In a duopoly environment, particularly where one of the licences is held by the operator of the PSTN, prices may be held at a level much higher than costs if a second operator takes the incumbent's prices as a benchmark in setting its own tariffs. Even in more openly competitive markets since 1992, new operators faced with relatively high start-up costs have taken the mobile duopolist's prices as a benchmark. This does not mean that this benchmark is fixed. In cases such as Japan, Sweden and the United Kingdom, the existing operators have lowered prices when faced with a third or fourth competitor but existing mobile prices, rather than the fixed network prices, are used as the benchmark for pricing. This situation will change in markets with multiple operators.

One driver of change is that the existing duopolists already have many of the most lucrative customers (*i.e.* high volume users) so that new operators need to expand their customer base to lower their unit cost. In other words new operators are not in a position to repeat the initial strategies of incumbents. For their services to be economic they have to evolve mobile communication into a 'mass market business' with a low unit cost per customer. While the market is growing very quickly for all operators, driven by tariff differentiation, there will be less pressure to compete on prices. Over time there will be greater pressure to compete on price and to develop new markets. It is at this stage that mobile operators will increasingly challenge the different PSTN markets for areas where they can compete. The first sign of this trend has been the pricing strategy pursued by One-2-One in the United Kingdom by adopting a regime of free calls in off-peak times and differentiating prices based on location for business users. The latter option means that business users can use their mobile telephone below the cost of the fixed network from a designated location (*e.g.* office), but pay standard mobile rates outside that place. In both these instances, designated location rates and free off-peak rates, mobile communication is acting as a competitor to the fixed network at certain times of the day and locations.[54]

A major caveat in any future scenario of the competitiveness of mobile networks with fixed networks is that PTOs can undoubtedly improve their performance. At one level this will occur as a consequence of ongoing improvements in network technologies such as switching and transmission and the economies this will enable. In the past, PTOs have had little incentive to be innovative in providing access technologies to customer premises. Indeed it is only since the opening of the local market in the United Kingdom that new technologies, such as fixed wireless and cable telephony, are being developed to lower the cost of access. Moreover fixed network operators can offer a greater range of services than mobile networks, so that for many customers the PSTN will remain the most attractive option. Alternatively the major market for PSTN services is voice telephony, a market readily accessible to wireless technologies. To date, however, and for the foreseeable future mobile networks have generated much more traffic and revenue for fixed networks than they have drawn away.

The available evidence already indicates that wireless networks are increasingly competitive on cost and this is reflected in the high profitability achieved by mobile operators. As the US Government Accounting Office has pointed out in an examination of mobile telecommunication pricing, if firms in duopolistic markets succeed in keeping prices above a competitive level, economic theory suggests that they will achieve a significant level of profitability.[55] In the main the profitability of mobile telecommunication has not been available for scrutiny. Most PTOs do not report separate results for mobile telecommunication. Often the first public indication of how profitable mobile operations are is when they are spun off from the PSTN operator. For example in 1994 Telecom Italia's mobile operations contributed L800 billion (25.9 per cent) out of a company wide pre-tax profit of L3 092 billion even though mobile subscribers were a fraction of PSTN subscribers.[56] The data in Table 25 show a wide cross section of profitability (operating income before tax as percentage of revenue). Established operators such as AirTouch and Vodafone are very profitable at their current levels of pricing, and their costs are lower than an average mainline cost on the PSTN, raising very interesting scenarios if new competitors force them to address new markets. Alternatively PSTN operators, and in particular those specialising in long-distance networks, may view wireless (fixed and mobile) as an increasingly attractive option to access customers.

The potential benefits for Member countries are very large in terms of lowering the costs of telecommunication for business and personal communication users and, over time, both improving and reducing the cost of providing universal service. It is being increasingly recognised that far greater costs are incurred by operators through inefficiency than in the provision of universal service. In future, mobile communication networks, to the extent that they act as a spur to increase PSTN efficiency, will lower the cost of universal service. On the other hand, as the costs of mobile telecommunication are reduced, the scope for using this technology to improve aspects of universal service to particular groups of people, such as the disabled or the elderly, will increase.[57]

Given the cost trends of different networks, the opportunity for such competition will increase but not without an appropriate regulatory framework. Experience has shown that mobile operators have been slow to address new markets unless they face an openly competitive market and that PTOs can use their monopoly power over the fixed network in ways that are antithetical to the efficient development of service. The available evidence indicates, both in terms of cost and profits, that it is timely to increase competitive pressure, particularly in monopoly and duopoly markets.

Table 20. **Fixed and mobile telecommunication costs in the United Kingdom**

	1986	1987	1988	1989	1990	1991	1992	1993	1994
BT's operating cost per mainline (£)	286	316	348	348	383	379	388	414	400
Vodafone's operating cost per subscriber (£)	1926	907	639	540	482	445	440	408	416
Vodafone's operating cost per subscriber (United Kingdom operations only) (£)	--	--	--	--	--	--	--	342	307

Source: Annual Reports, Vodafone Prospectus.

Table 21. **Fixed and mobile costs in Sweden**

	1991	1992	1993	Jan.- June 1994
Telia operating cost per mainline (US$ PPP) (1)	557	585	475	470
Telia Mobiltel operating cost per customer, (US$ PPP)	668	495	500	426

1. Net of mobile expense.
Source: Telia.

Table 22. **Fixed and mobile telecommunication costs in the United States**

	1990	1991	1992	1993	1994
Nynex operating cost per mainline (US$)	758	757	679	812	n.a.
AirTouch operating cost per subscriber (US$)(1)	819	776	733	645	544

1. PacTel Mobile data is used for 1990-91 and AirTouch domestic data for 1992-94.
Source: OECD, AirTouch, Nynex.

Table 23. **Fixed and mobile telecommunication costs in Germany**

	1992	1993	1994
Deutsche Telekom operating cost per mainline (US$)	851	954	n.a.
Mannesmann Mobilfunk operating cost per subscriber (US$)	2 543	1 264	1 164

Source: OECD, AirTouch.

Table 24. **BC Tel operating costs per mainline and mobile customer**

	1989	1990	1991	1992	1993	1994
Operating cost per mainline (C$) (1)	681	706	698	692	720	703
Operating cost per mobile customer (C$)	1 179	1 087	1 042	1 000	982	974
Ratio (per cent)	58	65	67	69	73	72

1. Net of mobile expense.

Source: BC Telecom.

Table 25. **Operating income as percentage of revenue in selected mobile communication operators**

Company	1985	1986	1987	1988	1989	1990	1991	1992	1993	1994
AirTouch				11.25	24.2	27.8	24.2	22.1	24.1	25.5
Alltel							11.3	16.6	22.0	26.3
BC-Tel					4.6	8.5	8.6	11.3	13.8	14.6
GTE				(1.7)	1.5	1.9	1.5	7.3	12.4	19.1
Mannesmann								(249.4)	(20.2)	12.9
McCaw						(4.1)	5.1	14.9	16.5	n.a.
Sonofon										(52.0)
Sprint								(0.8)	4.5	12.2
Tele-Mobil									17.3	n.a.
Telia							25.4	27.0	16.3	24.8
US Cellular							(16.9)	(7.7)	(3.5)	n.a.
Vodafone	(241.1)	(50.6)	(5.5)	26.8	35.0	40.5	45.5	46.3	48.9	42.6

1. Proportionate cellular data for AirTouch and McCaw.
2. 1994 data for Telia is a half-year figure.

Source: Annual Reports.

NOTES

1. The world-wide cellular subscriber base was estimated to be 52 million at the end of 1994. Refer *Mobile Communications International*, No. 21, April 1995, p. 67.
2. For example Dr Lars Ramqvist has predicted that by the year 2000 the world's telephone networks will be growing by about 100 million lines per year of which half will be personal mobile telephones but only if market forces prevail. Refer Lars Ramqvist, "Personal Communications in a Global Perspective", Ericsson Internet Home Page, 1995.
3. In some countries, such as Japan, Mexico and the United States, operators have been licensed on a regional basis. In this document, for simplicity, regional operators are considered to represent one national licence when there is a restriction on the number of operators in any one market.
4. OTE , the fixed network operator, was initially not permitted to operate a mobile network.
5. In February 1995, AirTouch purchased an 8.5 per cent interest in TeleZone, Inc. a Canadian consortium formed to pursue a 2 Ghz PCS licence. AirTouch expects the Canadian Government to award PCS licences in late 1995. Telezone currently uses the CT2-plus technology. MicroCell 1-2-1 is owned by a consortium including National Telesystem Ltd., Sprint Canada, Inc., FirsTel Communications Corporation, Phonespot Inc., and CUC Broadcasting Ltd.
6. "Broadband PCS Auction Nets US$7.7 Billion"; AT&T, Sprint, Bell Companies Win 70 of 99 Licences", *Telecommunications Reports*, 20 March 1995, p. 4.
7. OECD, *Telecommunication Infrastructure Competition: The Benefits of Competition*, ICCP No. 35, Paris, 1995.
8. In some countries PCS is referred to as personal communication networks (PCN) and personal handy phones (PHP). There is also a range of digital cordless telephone technology. In Canada, the standard chosen is CT2 Plus Class 2. For the sake of simplicity this report uses the term PCS to describe all these technologies. Other mobile cellular services are referred to as analogue (*e.g.* NMT) or digital service (*e.g.* GSM).
9. Spectrum issues were discussed by the ICCP and a report published entitled, OECD, *The Economics of Radio Frequency Allocation*, ICCP No. 33, Paris, 1993.
10. Refer to remarks of FCC Chairman Reed E. Hunt in "Broadband PCS Auction Nets US$7.7 Billion"; AT&T, Sprint, Bell Companies Win 70 of 99 Licences", *Op.cit.*

[11] In one study of demand for mobile communication, 64 per cent of companies interviewed nominated high call charges and 52 per cent high fixed charges as barriers to further use of cellular telecommunication. Refer Mari Vahanissi, "Integrating Mobility into the Corporate Network", *Mobile Communications International*, January 1995. p. 95

[12] Howard Ford, "It's a Big Boy's Game", *Mobile Communications International*, No. 21, April 1995, p. 32.

[13] Bell Mobility Canada, *Industry Fact Sheet*, 1995.

[14] Orange, *Price Guide*, Hutchinson Telecom, Bristol, November 1994.

[15] AirTouch Communications, Inc. "Securities and Exchange Commission Forum 10-K", 31 December 1994. p. 9. Prior to 1 April 1994, AirTouch was 86.1 per cent owned by Pacific Telesis. After this date the company was "spun off" and Telesis stock distributed to its shareholders.

[16] Ibid. "Management Discussion and Analysis of Financial Condition & Results of Operations", p. 22

[17] Flemmings Research, *Vodafone: Margins Reconsidered*, London, 3 March 1995.

[18] OECD, *The Economics of Radio Frequency Allocation*, ICCP No. 33, Paris, 1993. p. 17.

[19] Six new PCS licences were on offer. Two 30 MHz licences in each of the 51 Major Trading Areas and one 30 MHz licence and three 10 MHz licences in each of 493 Basic Trading Areas. The two existing cellular providers each have 25 Mhz of spectrum each. An operator is permitted to acquire up to 40 MHz in a single service area. Existing cellular operators are limited to obtaining an addition 10 Mhz in their service areas but are not under this restriction in other areas. Refer AirTouch, *Op.cit.* p. 10

[20] FCC, "FCC Grants Ten Regional Narrowband PCS Licences", 23 January 1995.

[21] OECD, *Communications Outlook 1995*, Paris, 1995, p. 98

[22] Ove Granstrand, "The Evolution of Nordic Mobile Telephony", International Telecommunications Society Conference, Stenungsbaden, Sweden, June 20-22, 1993. p. 20

[23] LM Ericsson, "Report on 1994 Operations", Ericsson Home Page, Internet, 9 March 1995.

[24] Kagan World Media, *International Cellular*, London, No. 35, 31 January, 1994.

[25] Kinnevik, *Annual Report, 1992*, Stockholm, 1992, p. 56

[26] Austel, *Quality of Service Bulletin*, Melbourne, March 1994.

[27] Case reported in OECD Secretariat interview with mobile service provider.

[28] Commission of the European Communities, *Towards the Personal Communications Environment: Green Paper on a Common Approach in the Field of Mobile and Personal Communications in the European Union*, Brussels, 1994. p. 117.

[29] John Blau, "German Competition in Sight", *Communicationsweek International*, 10 April 1995, p. 4.

[30] The Netherlands will also allow a future second operator to use its own infrastructure.

[31] Granstrand, *Op.cit.* p. 8.

[32] Pacific Telesis, *1992 Summary Annual Report*, 1993. pp. 3-4.

[33] S.G. Warburg Research, *The German Mobile Telephone Market*, London, October 1994, p. 10.

[34] Flemmings Research, *Vodafone: Margins Reconsidered, Op.cit.* p. 3.

[35] S.G. Warburg Research, *Op.cit.* p. 21.

[36] OECD, *Communications Outlook*, Paris, 1995.

[37] AirTouch, *Op.cit.* p. 15

[38] *Ibid.*

[39] LM Ericsson, "New Base Station Antenna Concept Extends Range and Cuts Costs for PCN (DCS 1800) Operators", Ericsson Home Page, Internet, 8 March 1995.

[40] S.G. Warburg Research, *Op.cit.* pp 20 - 22

[41] TOT (Telephone Organisation of Thailand) and CAT (Communications Authority of Thailand) are both state owned. TOT and CAT both in turn leased the rights to operate services to other operators including AIS (Advanced Information Services) and TAC (Total Access Communications) and these systems compete with their own. By 1994 there were four analogue service providers and two licences for GSM and DCS 1800 services had been awarded to AIS and TAC. For more information refer to the ITU, *World Telecommunication Development Report*, Geneva, 1994.

[42] Datapro, *Hong Kong: The Commercial and Regulatory Environment*, McGraw Hill, November, 1992.

[43] The average call charge is a composite of different call durations, time of day, and distances. Details can be found in OECD *Performance Indicators for Public Telecommunications Operators*, ICCP, No. 22, Paris, 1990. p. 48.

[44] The Company is a majority-owned subsidiary of Telephone and Data Systems, Inc. ("TDS"), an Iowa corporation.

[45] The information in this box is taken from the US Cellular's filings with the SEC.

[46] An exception would be Finland where local co-operative telephone companies charged high network joining fees but had lower rentals.

[47] US Cellular, *Op.cit.*

[48] OECD, "Mobile and PSTN Communications Services: Competition or Complementarity?", OCDE/GD(95)96, Paris, 1995.

[49] *Ibid.* p. 31.

[50] *Ibid.* p. 29.

[51] *Ibid.* p. 31.

[52] While BT's costs per mainline include the cost of Cellnet's mobile service, based on the Vodafone data, it would be expected to lower rather than increase average costs by 1994.

[53] LM Ericsson, "Visions of the Cellular Future", article authored 1994, Ericsson Home Page, Internet, 1995.

[54] For an examination of One-2-One's pricing refer OECD, *Telecommunication Infrastructure: The Benefits of Competition*, ICCP No. 35, Paris, 1995. pp. 60-62.

[55] GAO, "Concerns About Competition in the Cellular Telephone Industry", Report to the Honourable Harry Reid, Washington, July 1992.

[56] Flemmings Research, *Telecom Italia: How Much Upside from Cellular Spin-off?*, London, 22 March 1995, p. 2.

[57] OECD, *Telecommunication Infrastructure: The Benefits of Competition, Op.cit.* p. 26.

MAIN SALES OUTLETS OF OECD PUBLICATIONS
PRINCIPAUX POINTS DE VENTE DES PUBLICATIONS DE L'OCDE

ARGENTINA – ARGENTINE
Carlos Hirsch S.R.L.
Galería Güemes, Florida 165, 4° Piso
1333 Buenos Aires Tel. (1) 331.1787 y 331.2391
Telefax: (1) 331.1787

AUSTRALIA – AUSTRALIE
D.A. Information Services
648 Whitehorse Road, P.O.B 163
Mitcham, Victoria 3132 Tel. (03) 9210.7777
Telefax: (03) 9210.7788

AUSTRIA – AUTRICHE
Gerold & Co.
Graben 31
Wien I Tel. (0222) 533.50.14
Telefax: (0222) 512.47.31.29

BELGIUM – BELGIQUE
Jean De Lannoy
Avenue du Roi 202 Koningslaan
B-1060 Bruxelles Tel. (02) 538.51.69/538.08.41
Telefax: (02) 538.08.41

CANADA
Renouf Publishing Company Ltd.
1294 Algoma Road
Ottawa, ON K1B 3W8 Tel. (613) 741.4333
Telefax: (613) 741.5439
Stores:
61 Sparks Street
Ottawa, ON K1P 5R1 Tel. (613) 238.8985
12 Adelaide Street West
Toronto, ON M5H 1L6 Tel. (416) 363.3171
Telefax: (416)363.59.63

Les Éditions La Liberté Inc.
3020 Chemin Sainte-Foy
Sainte-Foy, PQ G1X 3V6 Tel. (418) 658.3763
Telefax: (418) 658.3763

Federal Publications Inc.
165 University Avenue, Suite 701
Toronto, ON M5H 3B8 Tel. (416) 860.1611
Telefax: (416) 860.1608

Les Publications Fédérales
1185 Université
Montréal, QC H3B 3A7 Tel. (514) 954.1633
Telefax: (514) 954.1635

CHINA – CHINE
China National Publications Import
Export Corporation (CNPIEC)
16 Gongti E. Road, Chaoyang District
P.O. Box 88 or 50
Beijing 100704 PR Tel. (01) 506.6688
Telefax: (01) 506.3101

CHINESE TAIPEI – TAIPEI CHINOIS
Good Faith Worldwide Int'l. Co. Ltd.
9th Floor, No. 118, Sec. 2
Chung Hsiao E. Road
Taipei Tel. (02) 391.7396/391.7397
Telefax: (02) 394.9176

CZECH REPUBLIC – RÉPUBLIQUE TCHÈQUE
Artia Pegas Press Ltd.
Narodni Trida 25
POB 825
111 21 Praha 1 Tel. (2) 242 246 04
Telefax: (2) 242 278 72

DENMARK – DANEMARK
Munksgaard Book and Subscription Service
35, Nørre Søgade, P.O. Box 2148
DK-1016 København K Tel. (33) 12.85.70
Telefax: (33) 12.93.87

EGYPT – ÉGYPTE
Middle East Observer
41 Sherif Street
Cairo Tel. 392.6919
Telefax: 360-6804

FINLAND – FINLANDE
Akateeminen Kirjakauppa
Keskuskatu 1, P.O. Box 128
00100 Helsinki

Subscription Services/Agence d'abonnements :
P.O. Box 23
00371 Helsinki Tel. (358 0) 121 4416
Telefax: (358 0) 121.4450

FRANCE
OECD/OCDE
Mail Orders/Commandes par correspondance :
2, rue André-Pascal
75775 Paris Cedex 16 Tel. (33-1) 45.24.82.00
Telefax: (33-1) 49.10.42.76
Telex: 640048 OCDE
Internet: Compte.PUBSINQ @ oecd.org

Orders via Minitel, France only/
Commandes par Minitel, France exclusivement :
36 15 OCDE

OECD Bookshop/Librairie de l'OCDE :
33, rue Octave-Feuillet
75016 Paris Tel. (33-1) 45.24.81.81
(33-1) 45.24.81.67

Dawson
B.P. 40
91121 Palaiseau Cedex Tel. 69.10.47.00
Telefax : 64.54.83.26

Documentation Française
29, quai Voltaire
75007 Paris Tel. 40.15.70.00

Economica
49, rue Héricart
75015 Paris Tel. 45.78.12.92
Telefax : 40.58.15.70

Gibert Jeune (Droit-Économie)
6, place Saint-Michel
75006 Paris Tel. 43.25.91.19

Librairie du Commerce International
10, avenue d'Iéna
75016 Paris Tel. 40.73.34.60

Librairie Dunod
Université Paris-Dauphine
Place du Maréchal-de-Lattre-de-Tassigny
75016 Paris Tel. 44.05.40.13

Librairie Lavoisier
11, rue Lavoisier
75008 Paris Tel. 42.65.39.95

Librairie des Sciences Politiques
30, rue Saint-Guillaume
75007 Paris Tel. 45.48.36.02

P.U.F.
49, boulevard Saint-Michel
75005 Paris Tel. 43.25.83.40

Librairie de l'Université
12*a*, rue Nazareth
13100 Aix-en-Provence Tel. (16) 42.26.18.08

Documentation Française
165, rue Garibaldi
69003 Lyon Tel. (16) 78.63.32.23

Librairie Decitre
29, place Bellecour
69002 Lyon Tel. (16) 72.40.54.54

Librairie Sauramps
Le Triangle
34967 Montpellier Cedex 2 Tel. (16) 67.58.85.15
Tekefax: (16) 67.58.27.36

A la Sorbonne Actual
23, rue de l'Hôtel-des-Postes
06000 Nice Tel. (16) 93.13.77.75
Telefax: (16) 93.80.75.69

GERMANY – ALLEMAGNE
OECD Publications and Information Centre
August-Bebel-Allee 6
D-53175 Bonn Tel. (0228) 959.120
Telefax: (0228) 959.12.17

GREECE – GRÈCE
Librairie Kauffmann
Mavrokordatou 9
106 78 Athens Tel. (01) 32.55.321
Telefax: (01) 32.30.320

HONG-KONG
Swindon Book Co. Ltd.
Astoria Bldg. 3F
34 Ashley Road, Tsimshatsui
Kowloon, Hong Kong Tel. 2376.2062
Telefax: 2376.0685

HUNGARY – HONGRIE
Euro Info Service
Margitsziget, Európa Ház
1138 Budapest Tel. (1) 111.62.16
Telefax: (1) 111.60.61

ICELAND – ISLANDE
Mál Mog Menning
Laugavegi 18, Pósthólf 392
121 Reykjavik Tel. (1) 552.4240
Telefax: (1) 562.3523

INDIA – INDE
Oxford Book and Stationery Co.
Scindia House
New Delhi 110001 Tel. (11) 331.5896/5308
Telefax: (11) 332.5993
17 Park Street
Calcutta 700016 Tel. 240832

INDONESIA – INDONÉSIE
Pdii-Lipi
P.O. Box 4298
Jakarta 12042 Tel. (21) 573.34.67
Telefax: (21) 573.34.67

IRELAND – IRLANDE
Government Supplies Agency
Publications Section
4/5 Harcourt Road
Dublin 2 Tel. 661.31.11
Telefax: 475.27.60

ISRAEL – ISRAËL
Praedicta
5 Shatner Street
P.O. Box 34030
Jerusalem 91430 Tel. (2) 52.84.90/1/2
Telefax: (2) 52.84.93

R.O.Y. International
P.O. Box 13056
Tel Aviv 61130 Tel. (3) 546 1423
Telefax: (3) 546 1442

Palestinian Authority/Middle East:
INDEX Information Services
P.O.B. 19502
Jerusalem Tel. (2) 27.12.19
Telefax: (2) 27.16.34

ITALY – ITALIE
Libreria Commissionaria Sansoni
Via Duca di Calabria 1/1
50125 Firenze Tel. (055) 64.54.15
Telefax: (055) 64.12.57

Via Bartolini 29
20155 Milano Tel. (02) 36.50.83

Editrice e Libreria Herder
Piazza Montecitorio 120
00186 Roma Tel. 679.46.28
Telefax: 678.47.51

Libreria Hoepli
Via Hoepli 5
20121 Milano Tel. (02) 86.54.46
Telefax: (02) 805.28.86

Libreria Scientifica
Dott. Lucio de Biasio 'Aeiou'
Via Coronelli, 6
20146 Milano Tel. (02) 48.95.45.52
Telefax: (02) 48.95.45.48

JAPAN – JAPON
OECD Publications and Information Centre
Landic Akasaka Building
2-3-4 Akasaka, Minato-ku
Tokyo 107 Tel. (81.3) 3586.2016
Telefax: (81.3) 3584.7929

KOREA – CORÉE
Kyobo Book Centre Co. Ltd.
P.O. Box 1658, Kwang Hwa Moon
Seoul Tel. 730.78.91
Telefax: 735.00.30

MALAYSIA – MALAISIE
University of Malaya Bookshop
University of Malaya
P.O. Box 1127, Jalan Pantai Baru
59700 Kuala Lumpur
Malaysia Tel. 756.5000/756.5425
Telefax: 756.3246

MEXICO – MEXIQUE
OECD Publications and Information Centre
Edificio INFOTEC
Av. San Fernando no. 37
Col. Toriello Guerra
Tlalpan C.P. 14050
Mexico D.F.
Tel. (525) 606 00 11 Extension 100
Fax : (525) 606 13 07

Revistas y Periodicos Internacionales S.A. de C.V.
Florencia 57 - 1004
Mexico, D.F. 06600 Tel. 207.81.00
Telefax: 208.39.79

NETHERLANDS – PAYS-BAS
SDU Uitgeverij Plantijnstraat
Externe Fondsen
Postbus 20014
2500 EA's-Gravenhage Tel. (070) 37.89.880
Voor bestellingen: Telefax: (070) 34.75.778

NEW ZEALAND – NOUVELLE-ZÉLANDE
GPLegislation Services
P.O. Box 12418
Thorndon, Wellington Tel. (04) 496.5655
Telefax: (04) 496.5698

NORWAY – NORVÈGE
NIC INFO A/S
Bertrand Narvesens vei 2
P.O. Box 6512 Etterstad
0606 Oslo 6 Tel. (022) 57.33.00
Telefax: (022) 68.19.01

PAKISTAN
Mirza Book Agency
65 Shahrah Quaid-E-Azam
Lahore 54000 Tel. (42) 353.601
Telefax: (42) 231.730

PHILIPPINE – PHILIPPINES
International Booksource Center Inc.
Rm 179/920 Cityland 10 Condo Tower 2
HV dela Costa Ext cor Valero St.
Makati Metro Manila Tel. (632) 817 9676
Telefax : (632) 817 1741

POLAND – POLOGNE
Ars Polona
00-950 Warszawa
Krakowskie Przedmieácie 7 Tel. (22) 264760
Telefax : (22) 268673

PORTUGAL
Livraria Portugal
Rua do Carmo 70-74
Apart. 2681
1200 Lisboa Tel. (01) 347.49.82/5
Telefax: (01) 347.02.64

SINGAPORE – SINGAPOUR
Gower Asia Pacific Pte Ltd.
Golden Wheel Building
41, Kallang Pudding Road, No. 04-03
Singapore 1334 Tel. 741.5166
Telefax: 742.9356

SPAIN – ESPAGNE
Mundi-Prensa Libros S.A.
Castelló 37, Apartado 1223
Madrid 28001 Tel. (91) 431.33.99
Telefax: (91) 575.39.98

Mundi-Prensa Barcelona
Consell de Cent No. 391
08009 – Barcelona Tel. (93) 488.34.92
Telefax: (93) 487.76.59

Llibreria de la Generalitat
Palau Moja
Rambla dels Estudis, 118
08002 – Barcelona
(Subscripcions) Tel. (93) 318.80.12
(Publicacions) Tel. (93) 302.67.23
Telefax: (93) 412.18.54

SRI LANKA
Centre for Policy Research
c/o Colombo Agencies Ltd.
No. 300-304, Galle Road
Colombo 3 Tel. (1) 574240, 573551-2
Telefax: (1) 575394, 510711

SWEDEN – SUÈDE
CE Fritzes AB
S–106 47 Stockholm Tel. (08) 690.90.90
Telefax: (08) 20.50.21

Subscription Agency/Agence d'abonnements :
Wennergren-Williams Info AB
P.O. Box 1305
171 25 Solna Tel. (08) 705.97.50
Telefax: (08) 27.00.71

SWITZERLAND – SUISSE
Maditec S.A. (Books and Periodicals - Livres et périodiques)
Chemin des Palettes 4
Case postale 266
1020 Renens VD 1 Tel. (021) 635.08.65
Telefax: (021) 635.07.80

Librairie Payot S.A.
4, place Pépinet
CP 3212
1002 Lausanne Tel. (021) 320.25.11
Telefax: (021) 320.25.14

Librairie Unilivres
6, rue de Candolle
1205 Genève Tel. (022) 320.26.23
Telefax: (022) 329.73.18

Subscription Agency/Agence d'abonnements :
Dynapresse Marketing S.A.
38 avenue Vibert
1227 Carouge Tel. (022) 308.07.89
Telefax: (022) 308.07.99

See also – Voir aussi :
OECD Publications and Information Centre
August-Bebel-Allee 6
D-53175 Bonn (Germany) Tel. (0228) 959.120
Telefax: (0228) 959.12.17

THAILAND – THAÏLANDE
Suksit Siam Co. Ltd.
113, 115 Fuang Nakhon Rd.
Opp. Wat Rajbopith
Bangkok 10200 Tel. (662) 225.9531/2
Telefax: (662) 222.5188

TUNISIA – TUNISIE
Grande Librairie Spécialisée
Fendri Ali
Avenue Haffouz Imm El-Intilaka
Bloc B 1 Sfax 3000 Tel. (216-4) 296 855
Telefax: (216-4) 298.270

TURKEY – TURQUIE
Kültür Yayinlari Is-Türk Ltd. Sti.
Atatürk Bulvari No. 191/Kat 13
Kavaklidere/Ankara
Tel. (312) 428.11.40 Ext. 2458
Telefax: (312) 417 24 90

Dolmabahce Cad. No. 29
Besiktas/Istanbul Tel. (212) 260 7188

UNITED KINGDOM – ROYAUME-UNI
HMSO
Gen. enquiries Tel. (171) 873 8242
Postal orders only:
P.O. Box 276, London SW8 5DT
Personal Callers HMSO Bookshop
49 High Holborn, London WC1V 6HB
Telefax: (171) 873 8416
Branches at: Belfast, Birmingham, Bristol, Edinburgh, Manchester

UNITED STATES – ÉTATS-UNIS
OECD Publications and Information Center
2001 L Street N.W., Suite 650
Washington, D.C. 20036-4922 Tel. (202) 785.6323
Telefax: (202) 785.0350

Subscriptions to OECD periodicals may also be placed through main subscription agencies.

Les abonnements aux publications périodiques de l'OCDE peuvent être souscrits auprès des principales agences d'abonnement.

Orders and inquiries from countries where Distributors have not yet been appointed should be sent to: OECD Publications Service, 2, rue André-Pascal, 75775 Paris Cedex 16, France.

Les commandes provenant de pays où l'OCDE n'a pas encore désigné de distributeur peuvent être adressées à : OCDE, Service des Publications, 2, rue André-Pascal, 75775 Paris Cedex 16, France.

1-1996

OECD PUBLICATIONS, 2, rue André-Pascal, 75775 PARIS CEDEX 16
PRINTED IN FRANCE
(93 96 01 1) ISBN 92-64-14789-6 – No. 48521 1996